SURVIVING YOUR FIRST YEAR OF TEACHING

Guidelines for Success

Richard D. Kellough
California State University, Sacramento

Merrill,
an imprint of Prentice Hall

Upper Saddle River, New Jersey   Columbus, Ohio

Editor: Debra A. Stollenwerk
Production Editor: JoEllen Gohr
Cover Photo: PhotoDisc., Inc.
Cover Design: Karrie M. Converse
Production Manager: Pamela Bennett
Director of Marketing: Kevin Flanagan
Marketing Manager: Suzanne Stanton
Marketing Coordinator: Krista Groshong

Printed in the United States of America

10   9 8 7 6 5 4 3 2

ISBN: 0-13-973835-5

Prentice-Hall International (UK) Limited, *London*
Prentice-Hall of Australia Pty. Limited, *Sydney*
Prentice-Hall of Canada, Inc., *Toronto*
Prentice-Hall Hispanoamericana, S. A., *Mexico*
Prentice-Hall of India Private Limited, *New Delhi*
Prentice-Hall of Japan, Inc., *Tokyo*
Simon & Schuster Asia Pte. Ltd., *Singapore*
Editora Prentice-Hall do Brasil, Ltda., *Rio de Janeiro*

TABLE OF CONTENTS

INTRODUCTION

I know of no profession that is potentially any more intrinsically rewarding than is that of teaching. However, for a public school classroom teacher, the first year of teaching or the beginning year at a new school can be extremely difficult. For a teacher without support, it can be overwhelming. Coupled with relatively low starting pay, it is little wonder that so many teachers become disenchanted with the profession and leave it within a few years.

By providing practical guidelines for the areas that concern most beginning teachers, it is my hope that this little book will provide a bit of a haven of help to prevent your becoming frustrated and discouraged. It is also my hope that it will aid in making your first year of teaching one that is intrinsically rewarding for you and emotionally and academically successful for you and your students.

As a teacher you are a learner among learners. You are beginning a career during which you will be in a perpetual mode of reflection and learning. Be kind to yourself; do not expect immediate mastery.

Karin Wescom, teacher at Elk Grove High School (CA), reminds me that perhaps the most important guideline of all is to value yourself and what you are doing. The first year is full of highs and lows, with few days in-between. There are days when you realize teaching is wonderful, and there are days where you are stressed to the max. Let yourself know when you're doing a good job, and remember that things can always improve.

Although guidelines presented in this booklet are mostly grade-level and subject-matter neutral, depending on your own particular teaching situation, you will personally find some to be more relevant than are others. Teaching is as much an art as it is a science; this is not a magic bag of recipes that will work for every teacher in every situation. As general guidelines for success during your first year of teaching, it does represent the best from recent research and from current practice. If you find that your interest is piqued by a particular guideline, you may learn more about that topic by referring to additional resources such as the readings listed in the back.

ASSESSING, GRADING, AND REPORTING STUDENT ACHIEVEMENT: TIME-INTENSIVE AND EXTREMELY IMPORTANT RESPONSIBILITIES

The development of the student encompasses growth in three domains—the cognitive, affective, and psychomotor. Traditional objective paper-and-pencil tests provide only a portion of the data needed to indicate student progress in learning. Various techniques of assessment should be used to determine how the student works, what the student is learning, and what the student can produce as a result of that learning.

While assessment of cognitive domain learning lends itself to traditional written tests of achievement, the assessment of learning within the affective and psychomotor domains is best suited by the use of performance rubric (standards) checklists where student behaviors can be observed in action. However, many educators today are encouraging the use of alternative assessment procedures (i.e., alternatives to traditional paper-and-pencil written testing). After all, for learning that is most important and that has the most meaning to students, the domains are inextricably interconnected. Learning that is meaningful to students is not as easily compartmentalized as the taxonomies of educational objectives would imply. Alternative assessment strategies include the use of group projects, portfolios, skits, papers, oral presentations, and performance tests. Performance rubric checklists can be prepared for use with any of these strategies.

Avenues for Assessing Student Learning

For assessing a student's achievement in learning, the three general avenues are (1) assess what the student *says*—for example, the quantity and quality of a student's contributions to class discussions; (2) assess what the student *does*—for example, a student's performance (e.g., the amount and quality of a student's participation in the learning activities); and (3) assess what the student *writes (or draws)*—for example, as shown by items in the student's portfolio (e.g., homework assignments, checklists, project work, and written tests). Although your own situation and personal philosophy will dictate the levels of importance and weight you give to each avenue of assessment, you should have a strong rationale if you value and weigh the three avenues for assessment differently than one-third each.

With each assessment strategy used, you are advised to proceed from your awareness of anticipated learning outcomes (the learning objectives) and to assess a student's progress toward meeting those objectives. That is assessment that is *criterion-referenced*.

When assessing a student's verbal and nonverbal behaviors in the classroom you should do the following:

1. Maintain an anecdotal record (teacher's log) book or folder, with a separate section in it for your records of each student.
2. For a specific activity, list the desirable behaviors.
3. Check the list against the specific instructional objectives.
4. Record your observations as quickly as possible following your observation. Audio or video recordings, and, of course, computer software programs, can help you maintain records and check the accuracy of your memory, but if this is inconvenient, you should spend time during school, immediately after school, or later that evening recording your observations while they are still fresh in your memory.
5. Record your professional judgment about the student's progress toward the desired behavior, but think it through before transferring it to a permanent record.
6. Write comments that are reminders to yourself, such as "Discuss observation with the student," "Discuss observations with student's mentor" (e.g., an adult representative from the community)," and "Discuss observations with members of the teaching team."

Assessing What a Student Says and Does. When assessing what a student says, you should (1) listen to the student's oral reports, questions, responses, and interactions with others and (2) observe the student's attentiveness, involvement in class activities, creativeness, and responses to challenges. Notice that I say you should listen and observe. While listening to what the student is saying, you should also be observing the student's nonverbal behaviors. For the latter, you will want to use observations with scoring rubrics of the student's performance in learning activities and periodic conferences with the student.

Assessing Student Writing. When assessing what a student writes, teachers use worksheets, homework, journal writing, writing projects, portfolios, and tests.

Student assignments and test items should correlate with and be compatible with specific instructional objectives (i.e., they should be criterion-referenced). Any given objective may be checked by using more than one method and by using more than one instrument. Subjectivity, inherent in the assessment process, may be reduced as you check for validity, comparing results of one measuring strategy against those of another.

Provide written or verbal comments about the student's work, and be positive in those comments. Rather than just writing "good" on a student's paper, briefly state what it was about it that made it good. Rather than simply saying or pointing out that the student didn't do it right, tell or show the student what is acceptable and how to achieve it.

Think First, Write Second: That Which Separates the Professional Teacher from Anyone Off the Street Is the Teacher's Ability to Go Beyond Mere Description of Behavior

Think carefully about any written comments that you intend to make about a student. Young people can be quite sensitive to what others say about them, and most particularly to comments about them made by a teacher.

Think before writing any comment on a student's paper, asking yourself how you believe the student (or a parent or guardian) will interpret and react to the comment and if that is a correct interpretation or reaction to your intended meaning.

I have seen anecdotal comments in students' permanent records that said more about the teachers who made the comments than about the recipient students. Comments that have been carelessly, hurriedly, and thoughtlessly made can be detrimental to a student's welfare and progress in school. Your comments must be professional; that is, they must be diagnostically useful to the continued intellectual and psychological development of the student. This is true for any comment you make or write, whether on a student's paper, or on the student's permanent school record, or on a message sent to the student's home. That which separates the professional teacher from anyone off the street is the teacher's ability to go beyond mere description of behavior. Keep that in mind always when you write comments that will be read by students, by their parents or guardians, and by other teachers.

Student Journals and Assessment

Avoid writing evaluative comments or grades in student journals. When reading student journals, talk individually with students to seek clarification about their expressions. Regardless of the subject that you teach, student journals are useful in understanding the student's thought processes and writing skills (diagnostic assessment) and should not be graded. For grading purposes, you may simply record whether the student is maintaining a journal and, perhaps, a judgment about the quantity of writing in it, but no judgment should be made by you about its quality. Student journals are for encouraging students to write (or draw), to think about their thinking (metacognition), and to record their creative thoughts. Encourage students to write about their experiences in school and out of school and especially about their experiences related to what is being learned. Encourage them to write their feelings about what is being learned and about how they are learning it. Writing in journals gives them practice in expressing themselves in written form and in connecting their learning and should provide nonthreatening freedom to do it. Comments and evaluations from teachers might discourage creative and spontaneous expression. When responding to a student's journal writing, Gibbs and Earley suggest that the following "don'ts" may be more important than any "do's":

- Don't correct spelling or grammar.
- Don't probe. Resist the temptation to ask for more than the student chooses to share.
- Don't respond with value judgments. Simple empathic statements, such as "I understand your point of view" and "Thanks for sharing your thoughts," can be used to avoid making value judgments.
- Don't require students to share their entries with you or their peers. Pages that students do not want you to read may be folded and marked "personal."[1]

Student Portfolios and Assessment

When reviewing student portfolios, discuss with students individually the progress in their learning as shown by the materials in their portfolios. As with student journals, the portfolio should not be graded or compared in any way with those of other students. Its purpose is for student self-assessment and to show progress in learning. For this to happen, students should keep in their portfolios all or major samples of papers related to the course.

Avoiding the Rush at the End of a Grading Period

If you are a secondary school teacher, by planning to end your own first and third quarter grading periods a week before the quarter ends, you can prevent the rush of having to read, score, and record

---

[1] L. J. Gibbs and E. J. Earley, *Using Children's Literature to Develop Core Values* (Bloomington, IN: Fastback 362, Phi Delta Kappa Educational Foundation, 1994).

papers, to convert scores to quarter grades for reporting, and to complete the reporting forms that must be turned in to the office. This may even be possible to do the second and fourth quarters.

ATTAINING CREDIBILITY WITH STUDENTS: TEACHER ATTITUDE AND MODELING BEHAVIORS

You probably don't need to be told that students enjoy and learn better from a teacher who is positive and optimistic, encouraging, nurturing, and happy rather than from a teacher who is negative and pessimistic, discouraging, uninterested, and grumpy.

In addition to being a positive and supportive teacher, to have a successful first year your behaviors should be consistent with, that is they must model, the behaviors expected of your students. A teacher whose behaviors are inconsistent with those expected of students quickly loses credibility with the students. For example, if you expect students to

- demonstrate regular and punctual attendance, then you should be punctual and regular
- have their work done on time, then you should do likewise returning their work promptly after reading, assessing, and recording it
- have their materials each day for learning, then you, too, must be prepared each day
- demonstrate cooperative behavior and respect for others, then you must do likewise
- maintain an open and inquisitive mind, to demonstrate critical thinking, and to use proper communication skills, then you will do likewise

BEYOND TEACHING: A TEACHER IS INTERESTING BECAUSE OF HIS OR HER INTERESTS OUTSIDE OF SCHOOL

Demonstrate an interest in the activities of the students and the many aspects of the school and its surrounding community. In addition, a wide range of interests outside of school will help you sustain your good health, energy, and enthusiasm for teaching. A teacher is interesting because of his or her interests; a teacher with varied interests more often motivates and captures the attention of more students. A teacher with no interests outside his or her subject and the classroom is likely a dull or soon-to-be burned out teacher.

First Year of Teaching: Not the Best Time to Assume New Personal and Social Commitments and Responsibilities

On the other hand, because you will be so busy, your first teaching year may not be the best time to begin graduate study or to take on major new social obligations and responsibilities. For example, you may want to think twice before planning a wedding or starting a family during your first year of teaching.

COLLEAGUES, ADMINISTRATORS, AND SUPPORT STAFF: YOUR PROFESSIONAL NETWORK

It is advisable to establish from the faculty at least one good friend. If you are a member of a teaching team, then at least one member of your team should be a friend with whom you can talk openly.

Two important persons at the school are the head custodian and the principal's secretary. If possible, include those persons in your network of professional friends. You will want to identify others at your school, such as cafeteria staff and campus security officers.

An Expert Among Professionals

Because of some special skill or knowledge, beginning teachers sometimes feel pressured to spend a great deal of time helping veteran teachers learn new skills or strategies. The request for help is made with the best of intention; it's just that veterans often have forgotten what the time demands on a beginning teacher can be like. For a new teacher who wants to be accepted, it is sometimes difficult to say no to requests. My advice: Be prepared for such requests and try to make time to help; just be careful to not overextend yourself. On the other hand, don't be afraid to say no; professionals will understand.

Envious Colleagues

Teachers who—because of their enthusiasm, energy, positivism, and fresh ideas—try to accomplish great things with their students are sometimes ostracized by envious colleagues. Unfortunately, in too many instances, after a few years, these creative teachers leave their respective schools and even the profession. Be prepared; if you are creative and enthusiastic about your teaching, there may be petty jealousy displayed by colleagues who are less enthusiastic, less successful, or burned out. My advice: Try to ignore them and focus on your students, your work, and, to the extent possible, surround yourself only with positive and supportive people.

Sharing a Common Purpose

The best schools and the best teachers provide a constructive and positive environment for learning and demonstrate optimism for the learning of every student.

For a student, nothing at school is more satisfying than having a teacher who demonstrates confidence in that student's abilities. Unfortunately, for some students, a teacher's show of confidence may be the only positive indicator that student ever receives. Each of us can recall with admiration a teacher (or other significant person) who demonstrated confidence in our ability to accomplish seemingly formidable tasks. A competent teacher demonstrates this confidence with each and every student. This doesn't mean that you must personally like every student with whom you will ever come into contact; it does mean that you accept each one as a person of dignity and who is worthy of receiving your respect and professional skills.

CURRICULUM CONCERNS

The accumulation of bits and pieces of information is at the lowest end of a spectrum of types of learning. For higher levels of thinking and doing, for learning that is most meaningful and longest lasting, the results of research support using (a) a curriculum where subjects are integrated and (b) instructional techniques that involve the learners in social interactive (student-centered) learning, such as cooperative learning, project learning, peer tutoring, and cross-age teaching.

Teaching Both Children and the Subject Matter Content Standards: An Oxymoron?

A concern of many beginning teachers (and experienced teachers, too) is that of discovering how to use more student-centered instruction (e.g., projects and group learning) as opposed to teacher-centered instruction (e.g., lecture and recitation) and still effectively teach the mandated or expected curriculum so that student achievement matches the expected outcome standards of the various content areas.

Elementary teachers in particular grapple for answers to the question of how to find the time to teach all the required content areas of the elementary school curriculum. At all levels—elementary, middle, and high school—teachers grapple with how to use more hands-on (i.e., doing it) and minds-on (i.e., thinking about what is being done) learning (which takes more time and materials) and still cover the expected and sometimes mandated curriculum. (By the way, doing it without thinking about it is not learning.) One key to success in accomplishing this seems to be via the use of some level of curriculum integration.

Integrating the Subjects

When speaking of curriculum integration, it is easy to be confused by the plethora of terms that are used but that seem related, such as *integrated studies, thematic instruction, multidisciplinary teaching, interdisciplinary curriculum,* and *interdisciplinary thematic instruction.* In essence, regardless of which of these terms is being used, the reference is to the same thing and that is to curriculum that is integrated. An integrated curriculum approach may not necessarily be the best approach for every school, nor the best for all learning for every child, nor is it necessarily the manner by which every teacher should or must always plan and teach. As evidenced by practice, the truth of this statement becomes obvious.

In attempts to connect students' learning with their experiences, efforts fall at various places on a continuum of sophistication and complexity, from the least integrated instruction (level 1) to the most integrated (level 5). What follows is to assist your understanding only; it is not my intention to imply that for every teacher or every program or school one level is any more appropriate or effective than another.

Level 1 curriculum integration is the traditional organization of curriculum and classroom instruction, where teachers plan and arrange the subject-specific scope and sequence in the format of topic outlines. If there is an attempt to help students connect their learning and their experiences, then it is up to individual classroom teachers to do it. A student who moves during the school day from classroom to classroom, teacher to teacher, subject to subject, from one topic to another is likely learning at a level 1 instructional environment. A topic in science, for example, might be "earthquakes." A related topic in social studies might be "the social consequences of natural disasters." These two topics may or may not be studied by a student at the same time.

If the same students are learning English/language arts, or social studies/history, or mathematics, or science, using a thematic approach rather than a topic outline, then they are learning at level 2 curriculum integration. At this level, themes for one discipline are not necessarily planned and coordinated to correspond or integrate with themes of another or to be taught simultaneously. The difference between what is a topic and what is a theme is not always clear. But, for example, whereas "earthquakes" and "social consequences of natural disasters" are topics, "natural disasters" could be the theme or umbrella under which these two topics could fall. At this level, the students may have some input into the decision making involved in planning themes and content.

When the same students are learning two or more of their core subjects (English/language arts, social studies/history, mathematics, and science) around a common theme, such as the theme "natural disasters," from one or more teachers, they are then learning at level 3 curriculum integration. At this level, teachers agree on a common theme, then they *separately* deal with that theme in their individual subject areas, usually at the same time during the school year. So what the student is learning from a teacher in one class is related to and coordinated with what the student is concurrently learning in another or several others. Some authors may refer to levels 2 or 3 as *coordinated curriculum*. At level 3, students may have some input into the decision making involved in selecting and planning themes and content.

When teachers and students do collaborate on a common theme and its content and when discipline boundaries begin to disappear as teachers teach about this common theme, either solo or as an interdisciplinary teaching team, level 4 integration is achieved.

When teachers and their students have collaborated on a common theme and its content, and discipline boundaries are truly indistinct during instruction, and teachers of several grade levels and of various subjects teach toward student understanding of aspects of the common theme, then this is level 5, an integrated thematic approach.

Cooperative Learning: Don't Give Up Before Experiencing Its Benefits

When they think they are using cooperative learning groups (CLGs), some teachers have difficulty and either give up trying to use the strategy or simply tell students to divide into groups for an activity and call that cooperative learning. However, for cooperative learning to work well, each student must be given training in and have acquired basic skills in interaction and group processing and must realize that individual achievement rests with that of their group.

As you probably know, the cooperative learning group is a heterogeneous group (i.e., mixed according to one or more criteria, such as ability or skill level, ethnicity, learning style, learning capacity, gender, and language proficiency) of three to six students who work together in a teacher- or student-directed setting, emphasizing support for one another. Often times, a CLG consists of four students of mixed ability, learning styles, gender, and ethnicity, with each member of the group assuming a particular role. Teachers usually change the membership of each group several to many times during the year. The theory of cooperative learning is that when small groups of students of mixed backgrounds and capabilities work together toward a common goal, members of the group increase their friendship and respect for one another. As a consequence, each individual's self-esteem is enhanced, and academic achievement is accomplished.

When the process of using CLGs is well planned and managed, the outcomes of cooperative learning include (a) improved communication and relationships of acceptance among students of differences, (b) quality learning with fewer off-task behaviors, and (c) increased academic achievement. In the words of Good and Brophy,

> Cooperative learning arrangements promote friendships and prosaic interaction among students who differ in achievement, sex, race, or ethnicity, and they promote the acceptance of mainstreamed handicapped students by their nonhandicapped classmates. Cooperative methods also frequently have positive effects, and rarely have negative effects, on affective outcomes such as self-esteem, academic self-confidence, liking for the class, liking and feeling liked by classmates, and various measures of empathy and social cooperation.[2]

For CLGs to work well, advanced planning and effective management are a must. Students must be instructed in the necessary skills for group learning. Each student must be assigned a responsible role within the group and be held accountable for fulfilling that responsibility. And, when a CLG activity is in process, groups must be continually monitored by you for possible breakdown of this process within a group. When a potential breakdown is noticed, you quickly intervene to help the group get back on track.

It is advisable to assign roles (specific functions) to each member of the CLG. The roles should be rotated, either during the

---

[2] T. L. Good and J. E. Brophy, *Looking in Classrooms* (New York: Longman, 1997), p. 278.

activity or from one time to the next. Although titles may vary, these are typical roles:

- *Group facilitator*—role is to keep the group on task
- *Materials manager*—role is to obtain, maintain, and return materials needed for the group to function
- *Recorder*—role is to record all group activities and processes and perhaps to periodically assess how the group is doing
- *Reporter*—role is to report group processes and accomplishments to the teacher and/or to the entire class. When using groups of four members, the roles of recorder and reporter can easily be combined
- *Thinking monitor*—role is to identify and record the sequence and processes of the group's thinking. This role encourages metacognition and the development of thinking skills.

It is important for students to understand and perform their individual roles, and it is important for each member of the CLG to perform her or his tasks as expected. No student should be allowed to ride on the coattails of the group. To give significance to and to reinforce the importance of each role, and to be able to readily recognize the role any student is playing during CLG activity, one teacher made a trip to an office supplier and had permanent badges made for the various CLG roles. During CLGs, then, each student pins the appropriate badge to her or his clothing.

Actually, for learning by CLGs to work, each member of the CLG must understand and assume two roles or responsibilities—the role he or she is assigned as a member of the group, and that of seeing that all others in the group are performing their roles. Sometimes this requires interpersonal skills that students have yet to learn or to learn well. This is where you must assume some responsibility, too. Simply placing students into CLGs and expecting each member and each group to function and to learn the expected outcomes may not work. In other words, skills of cooperation must be taught, and if all your students have not yet learned the skills of cooperation, then you will have to teach them. This doesn't mean that if a group is not functioning you immediately break up the group and reassign members to new groups. Part of group learning is learning the process of how to work out conflict. For a group to work out a conflict may require your assistance. With your guidance, the group should be able to discover what the problem is that is causing the conflict, then identify some options and mediate at least a temporary solution. If a particular skill is needed, then with your guidance students identify and learn that skill.

CLGs can be used for problem solving, investigations, opinion surveys, experiments, review, project work, test making, or almost any other instructional purpose. Just as you would for small group work in general, you can use CLGs for most any purpose at any time, but as with any other instructional strategy, it should not be overused.

Group Grading: Don't Do It

There are several techniques for using cooperative learning. Yet the primary purpose of each is for the groups to learn—which means, of course, that individuals within a group must learn. Group achievement in learning, then, is dependent upon the learning of individuals within the group. Rather than competing for rewards for achievement, members of the group cooperate with one another by helping one another learn, so that the group reward will be a good one. Normally, the group is rewarded on the basis of group achievement, though individual members within the group can later be rewarded for individual contributions.

Because of peer pressure, when using group learning you must be cautious about using group grading. For grading purposes, bonus points can be given to all members of a group; individuals can add to their own scores when everyone in the group has reached preset standards. The preset standards must be appropriate for all members of a group. Lower standards or improvement criteria could be set for students with lower ability or skills so everyone feels rewarded and successful. To determine each student's term grades, individual student achievement is measured later through individual student results on tests and other criteria, as well as through each student's performance in the group work.

Controversial Content and Issues: Unavoidable

Controversial content and issues, usually involving matters of religion, ethnicity, politics, gender, and sex, abound in certain disciplines, particularly in English/language arts (for example, challenged books—see Figure 1), social studies (for example, moral issues), and science (for example, the inclusion of creationism and biological evolution). As a general rule, if you have concern that a particular topic or activity might create controversy, it probably will. Throughout your teaching career, you will have to make decisions about how you will handle such matters. When anticipating content or an issue that might be controversial, consider the following guidelines.

A Day No Pigs Would Die (Robert Newton Peck)
The Adventures of Huckleberry Finn (Mark Twain)
Annie on My Mind (Nancy Garden)
The Arizona Kid (Ron Koertge)
The Catcher in the Rye (J. D. Salinger)
The Chocolate War (Robert Cormier)
Christine (Stephen King)
The Clan of the Cave Bear (Jean Auel)
The Color Purple (Alice Walker)
Diary of a Young Girl (Anne Frank)
Fallen Angels (Walter Dean Myers)
Flowers in the Attic (V. C. Andrews)
Forever (Judy Blume)
Go Ask Alice (Anonymous)
The Great Santini (Pat Conroy)
Grendel (John Gardner)
The Handmaid's Tale (Margaret Atwood)
I Am the Cheese (Robert Cormier)
I Know Why the Caged Bird Sings (Maya Angelou)
Lord of the Flies (William Golding)
Of Mice and Men (John Steinbeck)
The Outsiders (S. E. Hinton)
Romeo and Juliet (Shakespeare)
Running Loose (Chris Crutcher)
Scary Stories to Tell in the Dark (Alvin Schwartz)
Song of Solomon (Toni Morrison)
Tarzan of the Apes (Edgar Rice Burroughs)

Figure 1: Sample of books that have been challenged for use in public schools

Maintain a perspective with respect to your own objective, which is at the moment to retain your job and eventually obtain tenure. Probationary teaching is not necessarily the best time to make waves, to involve yourself in a situation that could lead to a lot of embitterment. If you communicate closely with your mentor (if you have one) and your department or grade level chair, you should be able to anticipate and prevent most problems of potential controversy.

Sometimes, however, during normal discussion in the classroom, a controversial topic will emerge spontaneously, catching you off guard. If this happens, think before saying anything. You may wish to postpone further discussion until you have had a chance to talk over the matter with members of your teaching team or other colleagues. Controversial topics can seem to arise most unexpectedly from nowhere for any teacher, and this is perfectly normal. Young people are in the process of developing their moral and value systems, and they need and want to know how adults feel about issues that are important to them, particularly those adults they hold in esteem—their teachers. Young adolescents and teens need to discuss issues that are important to society, and there is absolutely nothing wrong with dealing in the classroom with those issues as long as certain guidelines are followed.

Students should learn about not just one side but all sides of an issue. Controversial issues are open ended and should be treated as such. They do not have "right" answers or "correct" solutions. If they did, there would be no controversy. (An "issue" differs from a "problem" in that a problem generally has a solution, whereas an issue has many opinions and several alternative solutions.) Therefore, the focus should be on process as well as on content. A major goal is to show students how to deal with controversy and to mediate wise decisions on the basis of carefully considered information. Another goal is to help students learn how to disagree without being disagreeable—how to resolve conflict. To that end students need to learn the difference between conflicts that are destructive and those that can be constructive, in other words, to see that conflict (disagreement) can be healthy, that it can have value. A third goal, of course, is to help students learn about the content of an issue.

As with all lesson plans, one dealing with a topic that could lead to controversy should be well thought out in advance, during the planning stage of instruction. Problems for a teacher are most likely to occur when the plan has not been well prepared.

At some point, all persons directly involved in an issue have a right to input—students, parents and guardians, community representatives, and other faculty. This does not mean, for example, that people outside of the school have the right to censor a teacher's plan, but it does mean that parents or guardians and students should have the right without penalty to not participate and to select an alternate activity.

Although it is your decision, please understand that there is nothing wrong with students knowing your opinion about an issue as long as it is clear that the students may disagree without reprisal or academic penalty. However, it is probably best to wait and give your opinion only after the students have had full opportunity to study and report on facts and opinions from other sources. Sometimes it is helpful to assist students in separating facts from opinions on a particular issue by setting up on the overhead or writing board a fact-opinion table, with the issue stated at the top and then two parallel columns, one for facts, the other for opinions.

There is a difference between teaching truth, values, and morals, and teaching *about* truth, values, and morals. A characteristic that has made this nation great is the freedom for all its people to speak out on issues. This freedom should not be excluded from public school classrooms. Teachers and students should be encouraged to express their opinions about issues, to study the issues, to suspend judgment while collecting data, and then to form and accept each other's reasoned opinions.

You must realize, however, that as a university student it is not unusual to experience a professor who pontificates on a certain issue, as a public school teacher you do not necessarily have the same academic freedom. The students with whom you are working are not adults; they must be protected from dogma and allowed the freedom to learn and to develop their values and opinions, free from coercion from those who have power and control over their learning.

DECISION MAKING AND LOCUS OF CONTROL: NO ONE KNOWLEDGEABLE EVER SAID THAT GOOD TEACHING IS EASY, BUT IT IS FUN AND REWARDING

A teacher may make 3,000 nontrivial decisions every day.[3] Some decisions will have been made by you prior to meeting your students for instruction, others will be made during the instructional activities, and yet still others are made later as you reflect on the instruction for that day. Many of these decisions can and will affect the lives of students for years to come. You may see this as an awesome responsibility, which it is.

Coping Strategies

As a beginning teacher, you quickly become aware of the many responsibilities that rest on your shoulders and how alone you are when making the myriad of decisions every day. Life can be very lonely, especially if there is no one for you to approach when you feel frustrated or troubled and burdened by this responsibility. Thus, you

---

[3] C. Danielson, *Enhancing Professional Practice: A Framework for Teaching* (Alexandria, VA: Association for Supervision and Curriculum Development, 1996), p. 2.

need to identify a supportive and significant other with whom you can vent and talk over your concerns.

In addition, experienced teachers discover a variety of other ways to cope, such as deep breathing, physical exercising, getting away from school business, and reflecting. Incompetent teachers simply become aloof to the children and to their professional commitment and responsibility.

Decision Making

Instruction can be divided into four decision-making and thought processing phases. These are (1) the planning or *preactive phase*, (2) the teaching or *interactive phase*, (3) the analyzing and evaluating or *reflective phase*, and (4) the application or *projective phase*.[4] The preactive phase consists of all those intellectual functions and decisions you will make prior to actual instruction. The interactive phase includes all the decisions made during the immediacy and spontaneity of the teaching act. Decisions made during this phase are likely to be more intuitive, unconscious, and routine than those made during the planning phase. The reflective phase is the time you will take to reflect on, analyze, and judge the decisions and behaviors that occurred during the interactive phase. As a result of this reflection, decisions are made to use what was learned in subsequent teaching actions. At this point, you are in the projective phase, abstracting from your reflection and projecting your analysis into subsequent teaching behaviors.

Reflection and the Locus of Control

To continue working effectively at a challenging task (that is, to ease the stress of teaching) requires significant amounts of reflection. Writing reflections in a personal journal about your teaching and teaching experiences can be useful not only for easing the stress but also for improving your teaching. Following are sample reflective questions you might ask yourself:

- How did I feel about my teaching today?
- If I feel successful, what did I see the students saying and doing that made me feel that way? (If I do not feel successful, what did I see the students saying and doing that made me feel this way?
- Would I do anything differently next time? If so, what and why?

---

[4] A. L. Costa, *The School as a Home for the Mind* (Palatine, IL: Skylight Publishing, 1991), pp. 97-106.

• What changes to tomorrow's lesson need to be made as a result of today's?

It is while reflecting that you have a choice of whether to assume full responsibility for the instructional outcomes or whether to assume responsibility for only the positive outcomes while placing blame for the negative outcomes on outside forces (e.g., parents and guardians or society in general, peers, other teachers, administrators, and textbooks and materials, or lack thereof)—a lot of the latter can be heard while in the teacher's lounge. Where the responsibility for outcomes is placed is referred to as locus of control. Teachers who are intrinsically motivated and competent tend to assume full responsibility for the instructional outcomes, regardless of whether or not the outcomes are as intended from the planning phase.

DISCIPLINE: FEAR OF LOSS OF CONTROL IS A MAJOR CONCERN OF MANY BEGINNING TEACHERS

Effective teaching requires a well-organized, businesslike classroom in which motivated students work diligently at their learning tasks, free from distractions and interruptions. Providing such a setting for learning is called effective classroom management.

Essential for effective classroom management is the establishment and maintenance of classroom control, that is, the process of controlling student behavior in the classroom. Classroom control involves both steps for preventing inappropriate student behavior (the establishment aspect) and ideas for responding to students whose behavior is inappropriate (the maintenance aspect).

In a well-managed classroom, students know what to do, have the materials needed to do it well, and stay on task while doing it. The classroom atmosphere is supportive, the assignments and procedures for doing them are clear, the materials of instruction are current, interesting, and readily available, and the classroom proceedings are businesslike.

To be a successful classroom manager, you need to (a) plan your lessons thoughtfully and thoroughly, (b) provide students with a pleasant and supportive atmosphere, (c) establish control procedures that you can firmly and consistently apply, (d) prevent distractions, interruptions, and disturbances, and (e) deal quickly and unobtrusively with distractions and disturbances that are not preventable.

Beginning the School Year Well: Thorough Preparation Provides Confidence and Fosters Success

Beginning the school term well can make all the difference in the world. You should appear at the first class meeting (and every meeting thereafter) as well prepared and as confident as possible.

It is likely that every beginning teacher is to some degree nervous and apprehensive; the secret is to not appear to the students as being nervous. Being well prepared provides the confidence necessary to cloud feelings of nervousness.

Preventing a Ship from Sinking Is Much Easier Than Is Saving a Sinking One: Mistakes to Avoid

During your first year of teaching, no one, including you, should expect you to be perfect. You should, however, be aware of common mistakes teachers make that often are the causes of student inattention and misbehavior. It is my estimation that as much as ninety-five percent of classroom control problems are teacher-caused and preventable. In this section, you will find descriptions of mistakes commonly made by beginning (and even experienced) teachers. To have a most successful beginning to your career, you will want to develop your skills so to avoid these mistakes. To avoid making these mistakes requires both knowledge of the potential errors and a reflection upon one's own behaviors in relation to them.

As with all guidelines presented in this booklet, the items are mostly grade-level and subject-matter neutral, although clearly some may be more relevant to you than others, depending on your own particular teaching situation.

1. *Inadequately attending to long-range and daily planning.* A beginning teacher who inadequately plans ahead is heading for trouble. Inadequate long-term and sketchy daily planning is a precursor to ineffective teaching and, eventually, to teaching failure. Students are motivated best by teachers who clearly are working hard and intelligently for them.

2. *Emphasizing the negative.* Too many warnings to students for their inappropriate behavior—and too little recognition for their positive behaviors—do not help to establish the positive climate needed for the most effective learning to take place. Reminding students of procedures is more positive and will bring you quicker success than is reprimanding them when they do not follow procedures.

Too often, teachers try to control students with negative language, such as "There should be no talking," "No gum or candy in class or else you will get detention," and "No getting out of your seats without my permission." Teachers, too, sometimes allow students to use negative language on each other, such as "Shut up." Negative language does not help instill a positive classroom environment. To encourage a positive classroom atmosphere, use concise, positive language. Tell students exactly what they are supposed to do rather than what they are not supposed to do. Disallow the use of disrespectful and negative language in your classroom.

3. *Not requiring students to raise hands and be acknowledged before responding.* While ineffective teachers often are ones who are controlled by class events, competent teachers are in control of class events. You cannot be in control of events and your interactions with students if you allow students to shout out their comments, responses, and questions whenever they feel like it. The most successful beginning teacher is one who quickly establishes her control of classroom events.

In addition, indulging their natural impulsivity is not helping students to grow intellectually. When students develop impulse control, they think before acting. Students can be taught to think before acting or shouting out an answer. One of several reasons that teachers should usually insist on a show of student hands before a student is acknowledged to respond or question is to discourage students from the impulsive, disruptive, and irritating behavior of shouting out in class.[5]

4. *Allowing students' hands to be raised too long.* When students have their hands raised for long periods before you recognize them and attend to their questions or responses, you are providing them with time to fool around. Although you don't have to call on every student as soon as he or she raises a hand, you should acknowledge him or her quickly, such as with a nod or a wave of your hand, so the student can lower the hand and return to his or her work. Then you should get to the student as quickly as possible. Procedures for this should be clearly understood by the students and consistently practiced by you.

---

[5] For further reading about the relation of impulse control and intelligence, see D. Goleman, *Emotional Intelligence: Why It Can Matter More Than IQ* (New York: Bantam Books, 1995); and D. Harrington-Lueker, "Emotional Intelligence," *High Strides* 9(4):1, 4-5 (March/April 1997).

5. *Spending too much time with one student or one group and not monitoring the entire class.* Spending too much time with any one student or a small group of students is, in effect, ignoring the rest of the class. As a first-year teacher, you cannot afford to ignore the rest of the class, even for a moment.

6. *Beginning a new activity before gaining the students' attention.* A teacher who consistently fails to insist that students follow procedures and who does not wait until all students are in compliance before starting a new activity is destined for major problems in classroom control. You must establish and maintain classroom procedures. Starting an activity before all students are in compliance is, in effect, telling the students that they don't have to follow expected procedures. You cannot afford to tell students one thing and then do another. In the classroom, your actions will always speak louder than your words.

7. *Pacing teacher talk and learning activities too fast.* Pacing of the learning activities is one of the more difficult skills for beginning teachers to master. Students need time to disengage mentally and physically from one activity before engaging in the next. You must remember that this takes more time for a classroom of twenty-five or so students than it does for just one person, you. This is a reason that transitions (discussed later) need to be planned in your lesson plan.

8. *Using a voice level that is always either too loud or too soft.* A teacher's voice that is too loud day after day can become irritating to some students, just as one that cannot be heard or understood can become frustrating. You might benefit by asking a colleague to listen in on one of your classes to give you feedback about your voice. Some beginning teachers benefit from taking a speech class at a local university or community college.

9. *Assigning a journal entry without giving the topic careful thought.* If the question or topic about which students are supposed to write is ambiguous or obviously hurriedly prepared—without your having given thought to how students will interpret and respond to it— students will judge that the task is busywork (e.g., something for them to do while you take attendance). If they do it at all, it will be with a great deal of commotion and much less enthusiasm than were they writing on a topic that had meaning to them.

10. *Standing too long in one place.* Most of the time in the classroom, you should be mobile, "working the crowd."

11. *Sitting while teaching.* Unless you are physically unable to stand or you are teaching children in the early grades, in most situations as a beginning teacher there is no time to sit while teaching. It is difficult to monitor the class while seated. You cannot afford to appear that casual.

12. *Being too serious and no fun.* No doubt, good teaching is serious business. But students are motivated by and respond best to teachers who obviously enjoy working with students and helping them learn.

13. *Falling into a rut by using the same teaching strategy or combination of strategies day after day.* This teacher's classroom will likely become boring to students of upper grades. Because of the multitude of differences, students are motivated by and respond best to a variety of well-planned and meaningful learning activities.

14. *Inadequately using silence (wait time) after asking a content question.* When expected to think deeply about a question, students need time to do it. A teacher who consistently gives insufficient time for students to think is teaching only superficially and at the lowest cognitive level and is destined for problems in student motivation and classroom control.

15. *Poorly or inefficiently using instructional tools.* The ineffective use of teaching tools such as the overhead projector and the writing board says to students that you are not a competent teacher. Would you want an auto mechanic who did not know how to use the tools of her trade to service your automobile? Would you want a brain surgeon who did not know how to use the tools of her trade to remove your tumor? Like a competent automobile mechanic or a competent surgeon, a competent teacher selects and effectively uses the best tools available for the job to be done.

16. *Ineffectively using facial expressions and body language.* As said earlier, your gestures and body language communicate more to students than your words do. For example, one teacher didn't understand why his class of seventh graders would not respond to his repeated expression of "I need your attention." In one fifteen minute segment, he used that expression eight times. Studying a videotape of that class period helped him understand the problem. His dress was very casual, and he stood most of the time with his right hand in his pocket. At five foot, eight inches, with a slight build, a rather deadpan facial expression, and a nonexpressive voice, he was not a commanding presence in the classroom. Once he had seen himself on

tape, he returned to the class wearing a tie, and he began using his hands, face, and voice more expressively. Rather than saying "I need your attention," he waited in silence for the students to become attentive. It worked.

17. *Relying too much on teacher talk for classroom control.* Beginning teachers have a tendency to rely too much on teacher talk. Too much teacher talk can be deadly. Unable to discern between the important and the unimportant verbiage, students will quickly tune you out.

18. *Inefficiently using teacher time.* During the preactive phase of your instruction (the planning phase), think carefully about what you are going to be doing every minute, and then plan for the most efficient and therefore the most effective use of your time in the classroom. Consider the following example. A teacher is recording student contributions on a large sheet of butcher paper taped to the wall. She solicits student responses, acknowledges those responses, holds and manipulates the writing pen, and writes on the paper. Each of those actions requires decisions and movements that consume valuable time and can distract her from her students. An effective alternative would be to have a reliable student helper do the writing while she handles the solicitation and acknowledgment of student responses. That way she has fewer decisions and fewer actions to distract her. And she does not lose eye contact and proximity with the classroom of students.

19. *Talking to and interacting with only half the class.* While leading a class discussion, there is a tendency among beginning teachers to favor (by their eye contact and verbal interaction) only 40 to 65 percent of the students, sometimes completely ignoring the others for an entire class period. Feeling ignored, those students will, in time, become uninterested and perhaps unruly. Remember to spread your interactions and eye contact throughout the entire class.

20. *Collecting and returning student papers before assigning students something to do.* If, while turning in papers or waiting for their return, students have nothing else to do, they get restless and inattentive. Students should have something to do while papers are being collected or returned.

21. *Interrupting students while they are on task.* It is not easy to get an entire class of students on task. Once students are on task, you do not want to be the distracter. Try to give all instructions before students begin. Once on task, if there is an important point you wish to make, write it on the board. If you want to return papers while

students are working, do it in a way and at a time that is least likely to interrupt them from their learning task.

22. *Using "Shh" as a means of quieting students.* When you do that, you simply sound like a balloon with a slow leak. The sound should be deleted from your professional vocabulary.

23. *Overusing verbal efforts to stop inappropriate student behavior.* Beginning teachers tend to rely too much on verbal interaction and not enough on nonverbal intervention techniques. Verbally reprimanding a student for his or her interruptions of class activities is reinforcing the very behavior you are trying to stop. In addition, verbally reprimanding a student in front of his or her peers can backfire on you. Instead, develop your indirect, silent intervention techniques such as eye contact, mobility, silence, and proximity.

24. *Using poor body positioning in the classroom.* Develop your skill of "with-it-ness" by always positioning your body so you can continue visually monitoring the entire class even while talking to and working with one student or a small group of students. Avoid turning your back to even a portion of the class of students.

25. *Settling for less when you should be trying for more—not getting the most from student responses.* The most successful schools are those with teachers who expect and get the most from all students. Don't hurry a class discussion; "milk" student responses for all you can, especially when discussing a topic that students are obviously interested in. Ask a student for clarification or reasons for his or her response. Ask for verification of data. Have another student paraphrase what a student said. Pump students for deeper thought and meaning. Too often, the teacher will ask a question, get an abbreviated (often one word and low cognitive level) response from a student, and then move on to new content. Instead, follow up a student's response to your question with a sequence of questions, prompting and cueing to elevate the student's thinking to higher levels.

26. *Using threats.* Avoid making threats of any kind. One teacher, for example, told her class that if they continued with their inappropriate talking they would lose their break time. She should have had that consequence as part of the understood procedures and consequences and then taken away the break time for some students if warranted. In addition to avoiding using threats, be cautious about ever punishing the entire class for the misbehavior of some of the

students. Although the rationale behind such action is clear (i.e., to get group pressure working for you), often the result is the opposite of that intended—students who have been behaving well become alienated from the teacher because they feel they have been punished unfairly for the misbehavior of others. Those students expect the teacher to be able to handle the misbehaving students without punishing those who are not misbehaving, and they are right!

27. *Using global praise.* Global praise is pretty useless. An example is: "Your rough drafts were really wonderful." This says nothing and is simply another instance of useless verbalism from the teacher. Instead, be specific—tell what it was about their drafts that made them so wonderful. As another example, after a student's oral response to the class, rather than simply saying "Very good," tell what about the response was good.

28. *Using color meaninglessly.* The use of color, such as varying colored pens for overhead transparencies and using colored chalk, can be nice but will lose its effectiveness over time unless the colors have meaning. If you color-code everything in the classroom so that students understand the meaning of the colors, then use of color can serve as an important mnemonic to their learning.

29. *Verbally reprimanding a student across the classroom.* This is another example of the needless interruption of all students. In addition, it increases the "you versus them" syndrome, because of peer pressure. Reprimand, when necessary, but do it quietly and privately.

30. *Interacting with only a "chosen few" students rather than spreading interactions around to all students.* As a beginning teacher, it is easy to fall into a habit of interacting with only a few students, especially those who are vocal and who have significant contributions. Your job, however, is to teach all students. To do that, you must be proactive, not reactive, in your interactions.

31. *Not intervening quickly enough during inappropriate student behavior.* Inappropriate student behavior usually gets worse, not better, when allowed to continue. It won't go away by itself. It's best to nip it in the bud quickly and resolutely. A teacher who ignores inappropriate behavior, even briefly, is, in effect, approving it. In turn, that approval reinforces the continuation of inappropriate behaviors.

32. *Not learning and using student names.* To expedite your success, you should quickly learn the names and then refer to students by

their names when you call on them. A teacher who does not know or use names when addressing students is, in effect, seen by the students as being impersonal and uncaring.

33. *Reading student papers only for correct answers and not for process and student thinking.* Reading student papers only for correct responses reinforces the false notion that the process of arriving at answers or solutions is unimportant and that alternative solutions or answers are impossible. In effect, it negates the importance of the individual and the very nature of learning.

34. *Not putting time plans on the board for students.* Yelling out how much time is left for an activity, such as a quiz or small group learning activity, interrupts student thinking, in effect, saying their thinking is unimportant. As I have said before, avoid interrupting students once they are on task. In this instance, write on the board before the activity begins how much time is allowed for it. Write the time it is to end. If during the activity a decision is made to change the end time, then write the changed time on the board.

35. *Asking global questions that nobody likely will answer.* It is a waste of valuable instructional time. Examples are "Does everyone understand?" "Are there any questions?" and "How do you all feel about . . .?" If you truly want to check for student understanding or opinions, then do a spot check by asking specific questions, allow some time to think, and then call on students.

36. *Failing to do frequent comprehension checks (every few minutes in most situations) to see if students are understanding.* Too often, teachers simply plow through a big chunk of the lesson, or the entire lesson, only assuming that students are understanding it. Or, in the worst case scenario, teachers will rush through a lesson without even caring if students are getting it. Students are quick to recognize teachers who really don't care.

37. *Using poorly worded, ambiguous questions.* Key questions you will ask during a lesson should be planned and written into your lesson plan. Ask them to yourself or a friend, and try to predict how students will respond to a particular question.

38. *Trying to talk over student noise.* This simply tells students that their making noise while you are talking is acceptable behavior. All that you will accomplish when trying to talk over a high student noise

level is a sore throat by the end of the school day and, over a longer period of time, potential nodules on your vocal cords.

39. *Wanting to be liked by students.* Forget it. If you are a teacher, then teach. Respect will be earned as a result of your good teaching. Liking you may come later.

40. *Permitting students to be inattentive to an educationally useful media presentation.* This usually happens because the teacher has failed to give the students a written handout of questions or guidelines for what they should acquire from watching the program. Sometimes students need an additional focus. Furthermore, a media presentation is usually audio and visual. To reinforce student learning, add the kinesthetic, such as the writing aspect, when questions are used. This provides minds-on and hands-on activities that enhance learning.

41. *Beginning activities with stutter starts.* A stutter start is when the teacher begins an activity, is distracted, begins again, is distracted again, tries again to start, and so on. During stutter starts, students become increasingly restless and inattentive, making the final start almost impossible for the teacher to achieve. Avoid stutter starts. Begin an activity clearly and decisively.

42. *Introducing too many topics simultaneously.* It is important that you not overload students' capacity to engage mentally by introducing different topics simultaneously. For example, during the first 10 minutes of class a teacher started by introducing a warm-up activity, which was a writing activity with instructions clearly explained on the overhead; the teacher also verbally explained the activity, although she could have simply pointed to the screen, thereby nonverbally telling students to start working on the writing activity (without disrupting the thinking of those who had already begun). One minute later, the teacher was telling students about their quarter grades and how later in the period they would learn more about those grades. Then she went back to the warm-up activity, explaining it again. Next she reminded students of the new tardy rules (thereby introducing a third topic). At this time, however, most of the students were still thinking and talking about what she had said about quarter grades, few were working on the writing activity, and hardly any were listening to the teacher talking about the new tardy rules. There was a lot of commotion among the students. The teacher had tried to focus student attention on too many topics at once, thus accomplishing little and losing control of the class in the process.

43. *Failing to give students a pleasant greeting on Monday or following a holiday or to remind them to have a pleasant weekend or holiday.* Students are likely to perceive such a teacher as uncaring or impersonal.

44. *Sounding egocentric.* Whether you are or are not egocentric, you want to avoid sounding so. Sometimes the distinction is subtle, such as when a teacher says, "What I am going to do now is . . ." rather than "What we are going to do now is . . ." If you want to strive for group cohesiveness—a sense of "we-ness"—then teach not as if you are the leader and your students are the followers, but rather in a manner that empowers your students in their learning.

45. *Taking too much time to give verbal directions for an activity.* Students get impatient and restless during long verbal instructions from the teacher. It is better to give brief instructions (two or three minutes should do it) and get the students started on the task. For more complicated activities, you can teach three or four students the instructions for the activity and then have those students do "workshops" with five or six students in each workshop group. This frees you to monitor the progress of each group.

46. *Taking too much time for an activity.* No matter what the activity, think carefully about how much time students can effectively attend to the learning activity. A general rule of thumb for most classes (age level and nature of students and the activity will cause variation) is when only one or two learning modalities are involved (e.g., auditory and visual), the activity should not extend beyond about fifteen minutes; when more than two modalities are involved (e.g., add tactile or kinesthetic), then the activity might extend longer, say for twenty or thirty minutes.

47. *Being uptight and anxious.* Students quickly, consciously or unconsciously, detect a teacher who is afraid that events in the classroom will probably not go well. And it's like a contagious disease—if you are uptight and anxious, your students will likely become the same. To prevent such emotions, at least to the extent that they damage your teaching and your students' learning, you must prepare lessons carefully, thoughtfully, and thoroughly. Unless there is something personal going on in your life that is making you anxious, you are more likely to be in control and confident in the classroom when you have lessons that are well prepared. If you do have a personal problem, you need to concentrate on ensuring that your anger, hostility, fear, or other negative emotions do not adversely affect your teaching and your interactions with students.

Regardless of your personal problems, your classes of students will face you each day expecting to be taught reading, mathematics, history, science, physical education, or whatever it is you are supposed to be helping them learn.

48. *Failing to apply the best of what we know about how children learn.* Too many teachers unrealistically seem to expect success having all thirty-three students doing the same thing at the same time rather than having several alternative activities simultaneously occurring in the classroom (called multilevel teaching, or multitasking). For example, a student who is not responding well (i.e., being inattentive and disruptive) to a class discussion might behave better if given the choice of moving to a quiet reading center in the classroom or to a learning center to work alone or with one other student. If, after trying an alternative activity, the student continues to be disruptive, then you may have to try still another alternative activity. You may have to send the student to another supervised location (out of the classroom, to a place previously arranged by you) until you have time (after class or after school) to talk with him or her about the problem.

49. *Overusing punishment for classroom misbehavior—jumping to the final step without trying alternatives.* Beginning teachers sometimes mistakenly either ignore inappropriate student behavior or skip steps for intervention, resorting too quickly to punishment. They immediately send the misbehaving student outside to stand in the hall (not a wise choice because the student is unsupervised) or too quickly assign detention (a usually ineffective form of punishment). In-between steps to consider include the use of alternative activities in the classroom.

50. *Being inconcise and inconsistent.* Perhaps one of the most frequent causes of problems in classroom control for beginning teachers derives from their failure to say what they mean and mean what they say. A teacher who gives vague instructions and is inconsistent in his or her behaviors only confuses students; a teacher's job is not to confuse students.

Helping Students Develop Self-Control

Most successful teachers strive for student self-control. They do this by (a) clearly and concisely expressing their own expectations for student behavior and learning, (b) helping students establish a code of conduct for themselves, (c) helping students improve their own standards of conduct, (d) using a firm and consistent application of procedures and rules, and (e) quickly and unobtrusively refocusing an inattentive student to an on-task behavior.

EQUALITY IN THE CLASSROOM: ENSURE A PSYCHOLOGICALLY SAFE AND SUPPORTIVE LEARNING ENVIRONMENT

When conducting class discussions, it is easy to fall into the trap of interacting with only "the stars," or only those in the front of the room or on one side, or only the most vocal and assertive. To ensure a psychologically safe and effective environment for learning for every person in your classroom, you must attend to all students and try to involve all students equally in all class activities. Otherwise, ignored students may feel discriminated against and become inattentive and disruptive.

You must avoid the unintentional tendency of teachers of *both* sexes to discriminate on the basis of gender (or any other characteristic). For example, historically teachers have tended to have lower expectations for girls than for boys in mathematics and science. Teachers tend to call on and encourage boys more than girls. They often let boys interrupt girls but praise girls for being polite and waiting their turn. To avoid such discrimination may take special effort on your part, no matter how aware of the problem you may be. Guidelines for assuring equity in your classroom include:

- Avoid using gender-associated metaphors, such as "carry the ball" or "tackle the problem."
- During class instruction, insist that students raise their hands and be called on by you before they are allowed to speak out.
- Encourage students to demonstrate an appreciation for one another by applauding all individual and group presentations.
- Focus discussions on creative process thinking as well as on correct answers.
- Insist on politeness in the classroom. Insist that students be allowed to finish what they are saying, without being interrupted by others. Be certain that you model this behavior yourself.
- Keep a stopwatch handy to unobtrusively control the wait time given for each student to respond. Although at first this idea may sound impractical, it works.
- Maintain high expectations, although not necessarily identical expectations, for all students.
- Make every effort to call on boys and girls for their responses and contributions in equal ratio to their presence in your classroom.

FIRST DAY: YOUR ONE OPPORTUNITY TO MAKE AN INITIAL IMPRESSION

I cannot overemphasize the importance of (1) the first day of school, (2) the first week of school, and (3) the first few minutes of each class meeting. For you there will be just one opportunity to make a first impression on your students. The first few days of school set the tone for the entire year, and the first few minutes of each class meeting set the tone for the entire meeting.

On the first day you will want to cover certain major points of common interest to you and your students. The following are guidelines and suggestions for the initial meeting with your students.

Dress with Professional Pride

Dress for success. You are a professional; demonstrate pride in that fact. As cautioned by Niebrand, Horn, and Holmes, "If you dress, talk, and act like your students, they will see you as a peer or as someone trying to be their peer, and you will embark on a frustrating journey to self-destruction."[6]

Greeting the Students

Welcome the students with a smile as they arrive, and then greet the entire class with a friendly but businesslike demeanor. This means that you are not frowning, nor off in a corner of the room doing something else as students arrive. As you greet the students, tell them to take a seat and start on the first assignment already on each desk. Try to keep the class moving along at a fairly fast gait, without dead time (i.e., time when students have nothing to do).

Initial Activity

After your greeting, begin the first meeting immediately with some sort of activity, preferably a written assignment already on each student desk. This assures that students have something to do immediately upon arriving to your classroom. That first activity

---

[6] C. Niebrand, E. Horn, and R. Holmes, *The Pocket Mentor: A Handbook for Teachers* (Portland, ME: J. Weston Walch, 1992), p. 2.

might be a questionnaire each student completes. This is a good time to instruct students on the procedure for heading and turning in their papers. Collect the first assignment.

Student Seating

One option is to have student names on the first assignment paper and placed at student seats when students arrive that first class meeting. That allows you to have a seating chart ready on the first day, from which you can quickly take attendance and learn student names. Another option, not exclusive of the first, is to tell students that by the end of the week each should be in a permanent seat (either assigned by you or student selected), from which you will make a seating chart so that you can quickly learn their names and efficiently take attendance each day. Let them know, too, that you will redo the seating arrangement from time to time (if that is true).

Information About the Class

After the first assignment has been completed, discussed, and collected (allowing rehearsal of the procedure for turning in papers), explain to students about the course—what they will be learning and how they will learn it (covering study habits and your expectations regarding quantity and quality of work). Many middle school and high school teachers make a list of expectations or put this information in a course syllabus, give each student a copy, and review it with them, specifically discussing the teacher's expectations about how books will be used; about student notebooks, journals, portfolios, and assignments; about what students need to furnish; and about the location of resources in the classroom and elsewhere.

Procedures and Endorsed Behavior

Now, while you are on a roll, discuss in a positive way your expectations regarding classroom behavior, procedures, and routines. Young people work best when teacher expectations are well understood, with established routines. In the beginning, it is important that there be no more procedures than necessary to get the class moving effectively for daily operation. Five or fewer expectations should be enough, such as arrive promptly and stay on task until excused by the teacher, listen attentively, show mutual respect, use appropriate language, and appreciate the rights and property of others. Too many procedural expectations at first can be restricting and even confusing to students. As I said above, most students already know these things, so you shouldn't have to spend much time on the topic, except for those items specific to your course, such as dress and safety expectations for laboratory courses and physical education. Finding and applying the proper level of control for a given groups of students is a skill that you develop from experience.

Although many schools traditionally have posted in the halls and in the classrooms a list of prohibited behaviors, exemplary schools focus on endorsed attitudes and behaviors. For example, at Constellation Community Middle School (Long Beach, CA), all students receive regular daily reminders when after reciting the Pledge of Allegiance, they recite the school's five core principles:

1. Anything that hurts another person is wrong.
2. We are each other's keepers.
3. I am responsible for my own actions.
4. I take pride in myself.
5. Leave it better than when you found it.[7]

To encourage a constructive and supportive classroom environment, practice thinking in terms of "procedures" rather than of "rules," and of "consequences" rather than of "punishment." My reason is this: To many people, the term *rules* has a more negative connotation than does the term *procedures*. When working with a cohort of young people, some rules are necessary, but I believe using the term *procedures* has a more positive ring to it. For example, a classroom rule might be that when one person is talking, we do not interrupt that person until he or she is finished. When that rule is broken, rather than reminding students of the "rule," you can change the emphasis to a "procedure" simply by reminding the students, "What is our procedure (or expectation) when someone is talking?"

Although some experts disagree, it is my contention that thinking in terms of and talking about "procedures" and "consequences" are more likely to contribute to a positive classroom atmosphere than using the terms *rules* and *punishment*. Of course, some might argue that by the time students are in secondary school, you might as well tell it like it is. Like always, after considering what the "experts" have to say, the final decision is only one of many that you must make.

Once you have decided your initial expectations, you are ready to explain them to your students and to begin rehearsing a few

---

[7] D. Harrington-Lueker, "Emotional Intelligence," *High Strides* 9(4):1 (March/April 1997).

of the procedures on the very first day of class. Whichever, you will want to do this in a positive way. Young people work best in a positive atmosphere, when teacher expectations are clear to them, when procedures are stated in positive terms, are clearly understood and agreed upon and have become routine, and when consequences for behaviors that are inappropriate are reasonable and are also clearly understood.

What Students Need to Understand from the Start

As you prepare the expectations for classroom behavior, you need to consider some of the specifics about what students need to understand from the start. These specific points, then, should be reviewed and rehearsed with the students, sometimes several times, during the first week of school and then followed *consistently* throughout the school term. Important and specific things that students need to know from the start will vary considerably depending on whether you are working with third graders or tenth graders, and whether you are teaching language arts, physical education, or a science laboratory or shop class. But generally each of the following paragraphs describe things that all students need to understand from the beginning.

Signaling for your attention and help. At least at the start of the school term, most teachers who are effective classroom managers expect their students to raise their hands until the teacher acknowledges (usually by a nod) that the student's hand has been seen. With that acknowledgment, the student should lower his or her hand. The recommended procedure is that once their signal has been acknowledged by you, they are expected to return to their work.

Expecting students to raise their hands before speaking allows you to control the noise and confusion level and to be proactive in deciding who speaks. The latter is important if you are to manage a classroom with equality—that is, with equal attention to individuals regardless of their gender, ethnicity, proximity to the teacher, or another personal characteristic. I am not talking here about students having to raise their hands before talking with their peers during group work; I am talking about disallowing students shouting across the room to get your attention and talking out freely and impulsively during whole-class instruction.

An important reason for expecting students to raise their hands and be recognized before speaking is to discourage impulsive outbursts. One of the instructional responsibilities shared by all teachers is to help students develop intelligent behaviors. Learning to control impulsivity is one of the intelligent behaviors. Teaching children to control their impulsivity is a highly important responsibility that is too often neglected by too many teachers (and too many parents). To me, the ramifications of this are frightening.

To avoid student dependence on you and having too many students raising their hands for your attention, and to encourage positive interaction among the students, you may want to employ the "three before me" procedure. That is, when a student has a question or needs help, the student must quietly ask up to three peers before seeking help from you. As a beginning teacher, you need to try ideas and find what works best for you in your unique situation.

Entering and leaving the classroom. From the time that the class is scheduled to begin and until it officially ends, teachers who are effective classroom managers expect students to be in their assigned seats or at their assigned learning stations and to be attentive to the teacher or to the learning activity until excused by the teacher. This expectation works for college classes, for kindergarten, and for every level and class in between. For example, students should not be allowed to begin meandering toward the classroom exit in anticipation of the passing bell or the designated passing time, otherwise their meandering toward the door will begin earlier and earlier each day, and the teacher will increasingly lose control. Besides, it is a waste of a very valuable and very limited resource— instructional time. From the very first day, the procedure should be that you, not the bell, dismiss students.

Maintaining, obtaining, and using materials. Students need to know where, when, and how to store, retrieve, and care for items such as their coats, backpacks, books, pencils, and medicines; how to get papers and materials; and when to use the pencil sharpener and wastebasket. Classroom control is easiest to maintain when (a) items that students need for class activities and for their personal use are neatly arranged and located in places that require minimum foot traffic, (b) there are established procedures that students clearly expect and understand, (c) there is the least amount of student off-task time, and (d) students do not have to line up for anything. Therefore, you will want to plan the room arrangement, equipment and materials storage, preparation of equipment and materials, and transitions between activities to avoid needless delays and confusion. Problems in classroom control will most certainly occur whenever some or all students have nothing to do, even if only briefly.

Leaving class for a personal matter. Normally, older students should be able to take care of the need for a drink of water or to go to the bathroom between classes; however, sometimes they do not, or for medical reasons or during long block classes cannot. Reinforce the notion that they should do those things before coming into your classroom or during the scheduled times, but be flexible enough for the occasional student who has an immediate need. Follow established school procedures whenever you permit a student to leave class for a personal reason, which may, for reasons of personal security, mean that students can only leave the room in pairs and with a hall pass or accompanied by an adult.

Reacting to a visitor or an intercom announcement. Unfortunately, class interruptions do occur, and in some schools they occur far too often and for reasons that are not as important as interrupting a teacher and students' learning would imply. For an important reason, the principal or a vice-principal or some other person from the school's office may interrupt the class to see the teacher or a student or to make an announcement to the entire class. Students need to understand what behavior is expected of them during those interruptions. When there is a visitor to the class, the expected procedure should be for students to continue their learning task unless directed otherwise by you.

Arriving late to class or leaving early. You must abide by school policies on early dismissals and late arrivals. Routinize your own procedures so students clearly understand what they are to do if they must leave your class early (e.g., for a medical appointment) or when they arrive late. Procedures should be such that late arriving and early dismissal students do not have to disturb you or the learning in progress.

Consequences for Inappropriate Behavior

Teachers who are effective classroom managers routinize their procedures for handling inappropriate behavior to assure that students understand the consequences for inappropriate behavior. Consequences are posted in the classroom and, when not counter to school or team policy, may be similar to the five-step model shown in Figure 2.

Whether offenses subsequent to the first are those that occur on the same day or within a designated period of time, such as one week, is one of the many decisions you, members of your teaching team, department, or the entire faculty must make.

FIRST OFFENSE results in a direct but unobtrusive reminder (nonverbal warning) to the student.

SECOND OFFENSE results in a private but direct verbal warning.

THIRD OFFENSE results in the student's being given a time out in an isolation area (but one that has adult supervision) followed by a private teacher-student conference.

FOURTH OFFENSE results in a suspension from class until there is a student-parent-teacher (and perhaps the counselor) conference.

FIFTH OFFENSE results in the student being referred to the vice-principal or principal's or counselor's office (depending on school policy), sometimes followed by a limited or permanent suspension from that class or from school.

Figure 2: Sample model of consequences for student misbehavior

On the first day, you can point to the posted consequences and, depending on the age of your students, simply remind students of the consequences or explain them in some detail. But, don't spend an inordinate amount of time on the consequences; simply emphasize what they are and that they will be consistently enforced by you.

First Homework Assignment

End the first class meeting with a positive statement about being delighted to be working with them, and then give the first homework assignment. Make this first homework assignment one that will not take too much student time and one that each student can achieve a perfect score on with minimal effort. Be sure to allow yourself sufficient time to demonstrate where assignments will be regularly posted and to make assignment instructions clearly understood by every student, including a reminder of how you expect students to head their papers.

GUEST SPEAKER: HOW TO MAKE IT A SUCCESSFUL LEARNING EXPERIENCE

Bringing outside speakers into your classroom can be for students a valuable educational experience, but not automatically so. In essence, guest speakers are on a spectrum of four types, two of which should be avoided:

1. Ideally, a speaker is both informative and inspiring.
2. A speaker might be inspiring but have nothing substantive to offer. Except for the diversion it might offer from the usual rigors of classroom work, such an experience is a waste of valuable instructional time.
3. A speaker might be informative but be boring to students.
4. At the worst end of this spectrum is the guest speaker who is both boring and uninformative.

So, as for any other instructional experience, the bottom line is that to make the experience most effective takes careful planning on your part. The following guidelines are offered to make the experience most beneficial for student learning:

- If at all possible, meet and talk with the guest speaker in advance to inform the speaker about your students and your expectations for the presentation and to gauge how motivational and informative the speaker might be. If you believe the speaker might be informative but boring, then perhaps you can help structure the presentation in some way to make it a bit more inspiring. For example, stop the speaker every few minutes and involve the students in questioning and discussions of points made.
- Prepare your students in advance with key points of information that you expect them to obtain.
- Prepare students with questions to ask the speaker, things the students want to know, and information you want them to have.
- Follow up the presentation with a thank-you letter to the guest speaker and perhaps additional questions that developed during follow-up class discussions.

HIGH ENERGY DAYS AND THE DISRUPTION OF ROUTINE: KIDS ARE HUMAN, TOO

It is helpful to be aware of your moods and days of high stress, that is, to anticipate that your tolerance levels may vary. It helps to let your students know when your mind may be elsewhere or when your tolerance level for nonsense may be lower than normal.

Children, too, have days of high stress and anxiety. As you come to know your students well, you will be able to tell when certain students are experiencing an unusual amount of stress and anxiety, times when they may need extra listening and understanding. Many children come to school with so much psychological baggage that it is a wonder they come at all and can concentrate on school work when they do.

Understand that there are perfectly natural reasons why classroom routines are likely to be interrupted occasionally, especially on certain days and at certain times during the school year. Students will not have the same motivation and energy level on each and every day. Energy levels may also vary throughout the school day. Your anticipation of—and thoughtful and carefully planning for—periods of high or low energy levels will preserve your own mental health. Depending on a number of factors, including the age level and school, periods of high energy level might include the following:

- At the beginning of each school day
- Before a field trip, a holiday, or a school event—such as a dance, picture day, homecoming pep rally, or a school assembly
- On a holiday (such as Valentine's Day or Halloween)
- On the day following a holiday
- On a grade report day
- Immediately before lunch and immediately after lunch
- On a minimum day or the day a substitute teacher is present
- Toward the end of each school day
- Toward the end of school each Friday afternoon
- Toward the end of the school year, especially for seniors

In addition, although there may be no hard evidence, many experienced teachers will tell you that particular troublesome days for classroom control are those days when there is a strong north wind or a full moon. One teacher jokingly (I suspect) said that on days when there are both a strong north wind and a full moon, she calls in sick and for a substitute teacher.

What guidelines will help you prepare for these so-called high energy days? There are probably no specific guidelines that will work for all teachers in all situations in each instance from the list. However, these are days to which you need to pay extra attention during your planning. Students could possibly be restless and more difficult to control on these days, and you may need to be especially forceful and consistent in your enforcement of procedures or even compassionate and more tolerant than usual. Plan instructional activities that might be more readily accepted by the students. In no instance, however, do I mean to imply that learning ceases and play time takes over. What little instructional time is available to a teacher during a school year is too valuable for that to happen.

INTERNET: RESOURCE TO ENHANCE TEACHING AND STUDENT LEARNING

Originating from a U.S. Department of Defense project in 1969 (called ARPANET) to establish a computer network of military researchers, its successor, the federally funded Internet, has become an enormous, steadily expanding, worldwide system of connected computer networks. As you are probably well aware, the Internet provides literally millions of resources to explore, with thousands more added nearly every day. Only a few years ago, it was difficult to find any published information about the Internet. Today you can surf the Internet and find many sources on how to use it, and you can walk into most any bookstore and find hundreds of recent titles on using the Internet, most of which give their authors' favorite web sites. However, because new technologies are steadily emerging and because the Internet changes every day, with some sites and resources disappearing or not kept current, with others having changed their location and undergone reconstruction, and with new ones appearing, it would be superfluous for me to make too much of sites that I have found and can recommend as teacher resources. Nevertheless, Figure 3 is a listing of Internet resources that I have recently surfed, that have had some staying power, and that I recommend as potential resources for your teaching success.

• *Ask Dr. Math* (http://forum.swarthmore.edu/dr.math/dr-math.html), place to get answers to questions pertaining to mathematics
• *Beyond the MLA Handbook: Documenting Electronic Sources on the Internet* (http://falcon.eku.edu/honors/beyond-mla);
Citing Internet Addresses
(http://www.classroom.net/classroom/CitingNetResources.htm);
J. Walker's *MLA-Style Citations of Electronic Sources*
(http://www.cas.usf.edu/english/walker/mla.html)
• *Classroom Connect* (http://www.wentworth.com), resources for teachers; links to schools
• *Co-Vis Project* (http://www.nwu.edu/mentors/welcome.html), can match mentors with students to work on projects in science
• Cody's Science Education Zone
(http://www.ousd.k12.ca.us/~codypren/CSEZ_Home)
• *Council of the Great City Schools* (http://cgcs.org), descriptions of programs and projects in urban schools
• *Cyberspace Middle School*
(http://www.scri.fsu.edu/~dennisl/CMS.html), for students of grades 6-9 to get help in their education and work on science projects
• eDscape (http://www.edscape.com), for teaching ideas

- *Education World* (http://www.education-world.com), electronic version of *Education Week*
- *ENC* (http://www.enc.org), Eisenhower National Clearinghouse for Mathematics and Science Education; resources, activity guides, links to schools
- Encyclopedia Mythica (http://www.pantheon.org/mythica/)
- *ERIC Documents Online* (http://ericir.syr.edu), to search ERIC documents
- *FedWorld* (http://www.fedworld.gov), subject index to U.S. government; access to information from government agencies and departments
- *Global Schoolhouse* (http://www.gsh.org), ideas and lesson plans
- *Global Schoolnet Foundation* (http://www.gsn.org/), for resources and links for parents, teachers, and students from around the world
- *Globe Program* (http://www.globe.gov), an international environmental science and education partnership
- Health education (http://www.cpprev.org.)
- High School Database (http://www.writes.org/netscape/high_school-database/M.html), provides linkage to high school home pages
- Historical Text Archive (http://www.msstate.edu/Archives/History/index.html)
- History/social studies resources (http://www.execpc.com/~dboals/boals.html)
- Incredible Art Department (http://www.in.net/~kenroar), lessons and student art work
- Instructional technology clearinghouse (http://clearinghouse.k12.ca.us), sponsored by the State of California, provides recommendations on video, multimedia, and Internet-based resources
- *Kathy Schrock's Guide for Educators* (http://www.capecod.net/schrockguide/), resources and information
- *Language and Literacy Project* (http://www.uis.edu/~cook/langlit/index.html)
- *Learn the 'Net* (http://www.learnthenet.com), on using the Internet
- *Library of Congress* (http://lcweb.loc.gov/homepage/lchp.html), Civil War photographs, early motion pictures, legal information, and research sources
- Links to lesson plans, unit plans, thematic units, and resources (http://www.csun.edu/~hcedu013/index.html)
- Literature and humanities links (http://galaxy.einet.net/galaxy/Humanities/Literature.html)
- *MainFunction Sources for Education* (http://www.mainfunction.com), Microsoft's web site for distance learning and computer programming

- *Map Resources* (http://www.gsn.org/cf/maps.html)
- Math resources
(http://www-personal.umd.umich.edu/~jobrown/math.html)
- *Middle School Home Pages*
(http://www.deltanet.com/hewes/middle.html)
- Music Educator's Home Page (http://www.athenet.net/~wslow/); see
also (http://www.csun.edu/~vceed009/music.html) and
(http://www.jumpoint/com/bluesman/)
- *NASA Spacelink* (http://spacelink.nasa/gov/.index.html)
- *National Education Association resources for teachers*
(http://www.nea.org/resources/refs.html)
- National Service Learning Cooperative
(http://www.nicsl.coled.umn.edu)
- *National Service Learning Cooperative Clearinghouse*
(http://www.nicsl.coled.umn.edu)
- Native American resources
(http://hanksville.phast.umass.edu/misc/NAresources.html)
- *Newspapers in Education* (http://ole.net/ole/)
- PBS Mathline (http://www.pbs.org/learn/mathline/)
- Plane Math (http://www.planemath.com/)
- *School Match* (http://schoolmatch.com), directory of schools
- *School Page* (http://www.eyesoftime.com/teacher/index.html), a
teacher's resource exchange
- Science and Mathematics Resources
(http://www.hpec.astro.washington.edu/scied/science.html)
- *Shakespeare and the Globe: Then and Now*
(http://shakespeare,eb.com)
- Social Science Resources (http://www.nde.state.ne.us/SS/ss.html)
- *Study Web* (http://www.studyweb.com), place for students and
teachers to research topics
- Teacher's exchanges:
(http://www.education.indiana.edu/cas/tt/tthmpg.html);
(http://www.pacificnet.net/~mandel/);
(http://www.teachers.net/lessons/posts.html);
(http://www.teachnet.org) and (http://www.kidinfo.com)
- *Telementoring Young Women in Science, Engineering, and
Computing* (http://www.edc.org/CCT/telementoring)
- *The 21st Century Teachers Network* (http://www.21ct.org), network
of teachers helping teachers in education technology; see also
WWW4Teachers (http://4teachers.org)
- *U.S. Department of Education* (http://www.ed.gov/), for resources
and information
- *United Nations' CyberSchool Bus*
(http://www.un.org/Pubs/CyberSchoolBus/), for curriculum units and

projects, databases on U.N. member states, and global trends
- *United States Copyright Office* (http://lcweb.loc.gov/copyright)
- Weather (http://groundhog.sprl.umich.edu/); see also (http://www.fi.edu/weather)
- *Windows to the Universe Project* (http://www.windows.umich.edu), source of information on recent space research and discoveries
- Women's history (http://frank.mtsu.edu/~kmiddlet/history/women.html)
- World Wide Arts Resources (http://wwar.com/)

Figure 3: Internet resources

MAKEUP WORK: BE FIRM BUT UNDERSTANDING

Students will be absent and will miss assignments and tests, so it is best that your policies about late assignments and missed tests be clearly communicated to students and to their parents or guardians. Consider the following.

Homework Assignments

Although homework for students can be valuable and useful to their learning, it must be sensible, reasonable, and meaningful, or else it only alienates students (and parents). For example, there is no educational sense at all in all students doing identical assignments. There is no educational sense in assigning 20 problems to be done by a student who already knows how to do it. And, in too many instances, the school's treatment for students identified as being gifted is to simply overload them with homework. To the extent possible, for the greatest success, in the time that you have to do so try to individualize homework assignments. Regardless of anything else, avoid giving students what only amounts to meaningless busywork assignments.

Late Work: Consider All Aspects of a Student's Situation

I recommend as a general rule that after due dates have been negotiated or set for assignments, reduced credit or no credit be given for work that is turned in late. Sometimes, however, a student has legitimate reasons why he or she could not get an assignment done by the due date, and you must exercise a professional judgment in each instance. Although it is important that you have rules and procedures—and that you consistently apply those—you are a professional who should consider all aspects of a student's situation and, after doing so, show compassion, caring, and understanding of the human situation.

Tests and Quizzes

If students are absent when tests are given, you have several options. Some teachers allow students to miss or discount one test per grading period. Another technique is to allow each student to substitute a written homework assignment or project for one missed test. Still another option is to give the absent student the choice of either taking a makeup test or having the next test count double. When makeup tests are given, the makeup test should be taken within a week of the regular test unless there is a compelling reason (e.g., medical or family problem) why this cannot happen.

Sometimes students miss a testing period, not because of being absent from school but because of involvement in other school activities. In those instances, the student may be able to arrange to come into and take the test during another of your class periods, or your prep period, on that day or the next. If a student is absent during performance testing, the logistics and possible diminished reliability of having to readminister the test for one student may necessitate giving the student an alternate paper-and-pencil test or some other option.

Many teachers give frequent and brief quizzes, as often as every day. As opposed to tests, quizzes are usually brief (perhaps taking only five minutes of class time) and intended to reinforce the importance of frequent study and review. When quizzes are given at frequent intervals, no single quiz should count very much toward the student's final grade. Therefore, you will probably want to avoid having to schedule and give makeup quizzes for students who were absent during a quiz period. The following are reasonable options to administering makeup quizzes and are presented here in order of my preference, number one being my first choice:

1. Give a certain number of quizzes during a grading period, say 10, but allow a student to discount a few quiz scores, say two of the ten, thereby allowing the student to discount a low score or a missed quiz due to absence or both.
2. Count the next quiz double for a student who missed one due to absence. About the only problem with this option is when a student misses several quizzes in a row. If that happens, then try option three.
3. Count the unit test a certain and relative percentage greater for any student who missed one or more quizzes during that unit of instruction.

I advise against giving "pop" or unannounced quizzes; they serve no useful educational purpose. They only alienate students.

MEDIA: IF ANYTHING CAN GO WRONG, IT WILL!

When using media equipment, it is nearly always best to set up the equipment and have it ready to go before students arrive. That helps avoid problems in classroom management that can occur when there is a delay because the equipment is not ready. After all, if you were a surgeon ready to begin an operation and your tools and equipment weren't ready, your patient's life would likely be placed in further danger. Like any other competent professional, a competent teacher is ready when the work is to begin.

Of course, delays may be unavoidable when equipment breaks down or if a videotape breaks. Remember "Murphy's law," which says that if anything can go wrong, it will? It is particularly relevant when using audiovisual equipment. You want to be prepared for such emergencies. Effectively planning for and responding to this eventuality is a part of your system of classroom management and takes place during the preactive stage of your planning. That preparation includes consideration of the following.

When equipment malfunctions, keep three principles in mind: (1) you want to avoid dead time in the classroom; (2) you want to avoid causing permanent damage to equipment; and (3) you want to avoid losing content continuity of a lesson. So, what do you do when equipment breaks down? Again, the answer is, Be prepared for the eventuality.

If a projector bulb goes out, quickly insert another. That means that you should have an extra bulb on hand. If a tape breaks, you can do a quick temporary splice with cellophane tape. That means that tape should be readily available. If you must do a temporary splice, do it on the film or videotape that has already run through the machine rather than on the end yet to go through, so as not to mess up the machine or the film. Then, after class or after school, be sure to notify the person in charge of the tape that a temporary splice was made so that the tape can be permanently repaired before its next use.

If during brain surgery a patient's brain artery suddenly and unexpectedly breaks, the surgeon and other members of the surgical team are ready for that eventuality and make the necessary repair. If while working on an automobile a part breaks, the mechanic gets a replacement part. If, while teaching, a computer program freezes or aborts on the screen or if a fuse blows or for some other reason you lose power and you feel that there is going to be too much dead time before the equipment is working again, that is the time to go to an alternate lesson plan. You have probably heard the expression "Go to Plan B." It is a useful phrase; what it means is that without missing a beat in the lesson, to accomplish the same instructional objective or another objective, you immediately and smoothly switch to an alternate learning activity. For you, the beginning teacher, it doesn't mean that you must plan two lessons for every one but that when planning a lesson that utilizes audiovisual equipment, you should plan in your lesson an alternative activity, just in case. Then, you move your students into the planned alternative activity quickly and smoothly.

MOTIVATIONAL IDEAS: FOR YOUR REPERTOIRE

Today's youth are used to multimillion-dollar productions on television, videodiscs, arcade games, and the movie screen. When they come into a classroom and are subjected each day to something short of a high-budget production, it is little wonder that they sometimes react in a less than highly motivated fashion. No doubt, today's youth are growing up in a highly stimulated instant-action society, a society that has learned to expect instant headache relief, instant meals, instant gratification, instant communication, and perhaps, in the minds of many youth, instant high-paying employment. In light of this cultural phenomenon, I am on your side. The classroom teacher is on the firing line for six hours a day, five days a week, and is expected to perform, perhaps instantly and entertainingly, in a highly competent and professional manner, and in situations not even close to ideal. In any case, you must gain the students' attention before you can teach them.

In this section, you will find an annotated list of ideas. Although the ideas are organized according to subject fields and may or may not be appropriate for certain students or grade levels, I suggest that you read all entries for each field. Although one entry might be identified as specific to a particular field, it might also be useful in other areas. Or, it might stimulate a creative thought for your own stock of motivational techniques, such as an idea for a way to utilize the theory of multiple learning capacities or to emphasize the multicultural aspect of a lesson in math, social studies, or whatever the central discipline or theme of a lesson or unit of instruction.

The Visual and Performing Arts

1. As part of a unit on design, invention, or creativity, have students construct, design, and decorate their own kite. When the projects are complete, designate a time and place to fly the kites.

2. Use lyrics from popular music to influence class work, such as by putting the lyrics into images.

3. Invite a local artist who has created a community mural to speak to the class about the mural. Plan and create a class mural, perhaps on a large sheet of plywood or some other location approved by the school administration.

4. Use a mandala to demonstrate the importance of individual experience, as in interpreting paintings and in interpreting poetry.

5. Collect books, magazines, posters, films, videos, computer software programs, and so forth that show different kinds of masks people around the world wear. Ask students to identify the similarities and differences in the masks. Have them research the meanings that mask characters have in various cultures. Have students design and create their own masks to illustrate their own personalities, cultures, and so forth.

6. As part of a unit on the creative process, have each student draw or sketch on a piece of paper, then pass it on to the next person, and that person will make additions to the drawing. Instructions could include "improve the drawing," "make the drawing ugly," and "add what you think would be necessary to complete the composition."

7. Instructions for students: Imagine that you're a bird flying over the largest city you have visited. What do you see, hear, smell, feel, taste? Draw a "sensory" map.

8. Assign a different color to each student. Have them arrange themselves into warm and cool colors and explain their decisions (why blue is cool, etc.). Discuss people's emotional responses to each of the colors.

9. Watch videos of dances from various countries and cultures. Invite students to identify similarities and differences. Have students research meanings and occasions of particular dances.

10. Challenge students to discover ways in which music, art, and dance are used around them and in their community.

11. Find a popular song that students like. Transpose the melody into unfamiliar keys for each instrument. This makes the student want to learn the song, but in the process the student will have to become more familiar with his or her instrument.

12. Play a group-activity rhythm game, such as the "Dutch Shoe Game," to get students to cooperate, work together, and enjoy themselves using rhythm. Participants sit in a circle, and as the song is sung, each person passes one of his or her shoes to the person on the right in rhythm to the music. Shoes continue to be passed as long as verses are sung. Those with poor rhythm will end up with a pile of shoes in front of them!

13. Choose a rhythmical, humorous poem or verse to conduct as if it were a musical work. The students read the poem in chorus, while you stand before them and conduct the poem. Students must be sensitive to the intonation, speed, inflection, mood, and dynamics that you want them to convey in their reading.

14. Organize a Retired Senior Citizens Volunteer Program (RSCVP) with senior citizens presenting folk art workshops with students, and where then the students and seniors work together to create artworks for the school and community.

15. Organize students into making tray favors, napkin rings, placemats, door decorations, cards, and treat cups for the residents of a local veterans' home, convalescent center, or retirement home.

Family and Consumer Economics, Foods, and Textiles

16. Often the foods we like originated from another part of our country or the world. Have students identify such foods and from where they came: spaghetti, enchiladas, fajitas, wontons, tacos, quiches, croissants, teriyaki, fried rice, pizza, hot dogs, hamburgers, noodles, tomatoes, chocolate, potatoes, hoagies, chop suey, ice cream cones, submarines, poor boys. Have students list the names and origins and place pictures of the food in place on a large world map.

17. Take photos of class members at special events such as dinners, fashion shows, field trips, and special projects. Build a scrapbook or bulletin board with these and display on campus or at "Open House."

18. Plan thematic units on cultural foods, using the traditions, costumes, and music of a particular culture. Have the students decorate the room. Invite the principal for a meal and visit.

19. Have a committee of students plan and create a school hallway display of pictures of 100-calorie portions of basic nutritional foods and popular fad foods that contain only empty calories.

20. Pin the names of different garments on the backs of students. The students are then to sort themselves into different wash loads.

21. For a clothing unit, hold an "idea day." Ask each student to bring in an idea of something that can be done to give clothes a new look, a fun touch, or an extended wearing life. Their ideas may include appliqués, embroidery, tie-dye, batik, colorful patches, and restyling old clothes into current or creative fashions.

22. Have the students write, practice, and present skits on consumer fraud.

23. Once a month, have students plan a menu, prepare the food, and serve it to invited senior citizens from the community.

24. Organize a program with senior citizens and students working together on a community garden.

25. Plan a program at a senior citizens' center whereby students and seniors work together on planning and decorating the center for special occasions and holidays.

26. Have students work on a project about culture and how culture affects the way we live. They learn that cultural differences can effect how an individual dresses, eats, worships, celebrates, and communicates.

27. Organize a program whereby students provide child care, cross-age tutoring, and companionship to preschool, elementary school, and elderly clients at off-campus locations.

28. Charge students with educating the school and local community about general nutrition and exercise.

English, Languages, and the Language Arts

29. Organize a paper or electronic letter writing activity between senior citizens in the community and your students.

30. For a unit on the Renaissance, creation of a wall-to-wall mural depicting a village of the times may be a total team project. Students can research customs, costumes, and architecture. Others may paint or draw.

31. On a road map, have students find the names of places that sound "foreign" and categorize the names according to nationality or culture.

32. To enhance understanding of parts of speech, set up this problem: Provide several boxes containing different parts of speech. Each student is to form one sentence from the fragments chosen from each box, being allowed to discard only at a penalty. The students then nonverbally make trades with other students to make coherent and perhaps meaningfully amusing sentences. A student may trade a noun for a verb but will have to keep in mind what parts of speech are essential for a sentence. Results may be read aloud as a culmination to this activity.

33. Students can match American English and British English words (or any other combination of languages), such as cookies and biscuits; hood and bonnet; canned meat and tinned meat; elevator and lift; flashlight and torch; subway and tube; garbage collector and dustman; undershirt and vest; sweater and jumper; and gasoline and petrol. Have students compare pronunciations and spellings.

34. English words derive from many other languages. Have students list some, such as ketchup (Malay), alcohol (Arabic), kindergarten (German), menu (French), shampoo (Hindi), bonanza (Spanish), piano (Italian), kosher (Yiddish), and smorgasbord (Swedish).

35. For an exercise in objective versus subjective writing, after a lesson on descriptive writing, bring to the class a nondescript object, such as a potato, and place it before the class. Ask them to write a paragraph either describing the potato in detail, that is, its color, size, markings, and other characteristics, or describing how the potato feels about them.

36. Read a story to the class but leave out the ending. Then ask the students (as individuals or in think-write-share pairs) to create and write their own endings or conclusions.

37. Invite students to create an advertisement using a propaganda device of their choice.

38. Invite students (individually or in pairs) to create and design an invention and then to write a "patent description" for the invention.

39. Using think-write-share pairs, invite students to write a physical description of some well-known public figure, such as a movie star, politician, athlete, or musician. Other class members may enjoy trying to identify the "mystery" personality from the written description.

40. A bulletin board may be designated for current events and news in the world of writers. Included may be new books and recordings as well as reviews. News of poets and authors (student authors and poets, too) may also be displayed.

41. Everyone has heard of or experienced stereotyping, for example, girls are not as athletic as boys, boys are insensitive, women are better cooks than men, men are more mechanical than women. Ask students to list some stereotypes they have heard and examples they find in newspapers, magazines, movies, and television. Have students discuss these questions: How do you suppose these stereotypes came to be? Does stereotyping have any useful value? Is it sometimes harmful?

42. Remove the text from a Sunday newspaper comic strip and have the students work in pairs to create the story line; or give each pair a picture from a magazine and have the pair create a story about the picture.

43. Use newspaper want ads to locate jobs as a base for completing job application forms and creating letters of inquiry. Use videotape equipment to record employer-employee role-play situations, interviews for jobs, or child-parent situations, to develop language and listening skills.

44. Invite students to choose a short story from a text and to write it into a play and perform the play for parents.

45. When beginning a poetry unit, ask students to bring in the words to their favorite songs. Show how these fit into the genre of poetry.

46. Invite students to look for commercial examples of advertisements that might be classed as "eco-pornographic," that is, ads for a product that is potentially damaging to our environment. Or, have students analyze advertisements for the emotions they appeal to, for the techniques used, and for their integrity. Try the same thing with radio, youth magazines, and other media.

47. Change the learning environment by moving to an outdoor location, and ask students to write poetry to see if the change in surroundings stimulates or discourages their creativeness. Discuss the results. For example, take your class to a large supermarket to write, or to a lake, or into a forest, or to the school athletic stadium.

48. To introduce the concept of interpretations, use your state's seal to start the study. Have students analyze the seal for its history and the meaning of its various symbols.

49. When learning a language, provide puppets in native costume for students to use in practicing dialogue.

50. Use the Internet to establish communication with students from another area of the country or world; establish a Web page for your school.

51. Use drama to build language arts and thinking skills. Have students write dialogue, set scenes, and communicate emotions through expressive language and mime.

Mathematics

52. Collaboratively plan with students a role-play unit where members role-play the solar system. Students calculate their weights, set up a proportion system, find a large field, and on the final day actually simulate the solar system, using their own bodies to represent the sun, planets, and moons. Arrange to have the event photographed.

53. Encourage students to look for evidence of Fibonacci number series (i.e., 1, 1, 2, 3, 5, 8, 13, 21, etc.), outside of mathematics, such as in nature and in manufactured objects. Here are examples of where evidence may be found: piano keyboard, petals on flowers,

spermatogenesis, and oogenesis. Perhaps your students might like to organize a Fibonacci club and through the Internet establish communication with other clubs around the world.

54. Give students the history of cost of a first-class U.S. postage stamp, and ask the students to devise ways of predicting its cost by the year they graduate, the year they become grandparents, or some other target year.

55. Give students a list of the frequencies of each of the 88 keys and strings of a piano (a local music store can provide the information). Challenge students to derive an equation to express the relation between key position and frequency. After they have does this, research and tell them about the Bösendorfer piano (Germany) with its nine extra keys at the lower end of the keyboard. See if students can predict the frequencies of those extra keys.

56. Using a light sensor to measure the intensity of a light source from various distances, have students graph the data points and then, with their scientific calculators, find the relevant equation.

Science

57. Challenge students to create and test their own science tools and materials, such as microscopes using bamboo rods with a drop of water in each end or litmus indicators using the petals of flowers or cosmetics.

58. Use cassette-tape recorders to record sounds of the environment. Compare and write about day and night sounds.

59. With appropriate permissions, plan an overnight campout in which the students must "live off the land" with only sleeping bags, clothing, and other essentials, but with no electronics.

60. Plan a year-long project where each student, or small group of students, must develop knowledge and understanding of some specific piece of technology. Each project culmination presentation must have five components: visual, oral, written, artistic, and creative.

61. Have students in an inner-city school use landlord-tenant situations to develop a role-play simulation of predator-prey relationships.

62. If you are a teacher of life science, make sure your classroom looks like a place for the study of the living rather than of the dead. A life science classroom that contains only a variety of dust-covered jars of pickled specimens probably belongs to a dust-covered teacher who acts as if he or she is one of those specimens.

63. With each student playing the role of a cell part, have students set up and perform a dramatic role-play of cells.

64. Divide the class of students into groups, and ask each group to create an environment for an imaginary animal using discarded items from the environment. By asking questions, each group will try to learn about other groups' "mystery" animals.

65. Have each student, or student pair, "adopt" a chemical element. The student then researches that element and becomes the class expert whenever that particular substance comes up in discussion. There could be a special bulletin board for putting up questions on interesting or little-known facts about the elements.

66. Milk can be precipitated, separated, and the solid product dried to form a very hard substance that was, in the days before plastic, used to make buttons. Let students make their own buttons from milk.

67. As a class or interdisciplinary team project, obtain permission and "adopt" a wetlands area or some other environmental project near the school. For example, students at Baldwyn Middle School (Baldwyn, MS) planned and cared for the landscaping of the local battlefield/museum.

68. Invite students to research the composition and development of familiar objects. For example, an ordinary pencil is made of cedar wood from the forests of the Pacific Northwest. The graphite is often from Montana or Mexico and is reinforced with clays from Georgia and Kentucky. The eraser is made from soybean oil and latex from trees in South America, reinforced with pumice from California or New Mexico, and sulfur, calcium, and barium. The metal band is aluminum or brass, made from copper and zinc mined in no fewer than 13 states and nine provinces of Canada. The paint to color the wood and the lacquer to make it shine are made from a variety of different minerals and metals, as is the glue that holds the wood together.

69. Invite students to locate and design large posters to hang on the classroom walls that show the meaning of words used in science that are not typical of their meaning in everyday language usage.

70. To bridge cross-cultural differences, allow students to design large posters to hang on the classroom walls showing potential differences in perceptions or views according to ethnoscience and formal science.

71. At Great Falls Middle School (Montague, MA), students research and produce television documentaries on subjects related to energy. The documentaries are broadcast on the local cable channel to promote energy literacy in the school and community.

Social Sciences

72. Organize an Intergenerational Advocacy program, in which students and senior citizens work together to make a better society for both groups.[8]

73. Develop a year-long three-stage project. During the first stage, students individually research the question, "Who Am I?"; during the second stage, "Who Are They?"; third stage, "Who Are We?" Multimedia presentations should be part of the students' culminating presentations.

74. During their study of ancient Egypt, invite students to create and build their own pyramids; in science, students could study simple machines that will help them to build the pyramids.

75. Invite students to plan how they would improve their living environment, beginning with the classroom, then moving out to the school, home, and community.

76. Start a pictorial essay on the development and/or changes of a given area in your community, such as a major corner or block adjacent to the school. This study project could continue for years and have many social, political, and economic implications.

77. Start a folk hero study. Each year ask, "What prominent human being who has lived during (a particular period of time) do you most

---

[8] See, for example, D. E. MacBain, *Intergenerational Education Programs* (Bloomington, IN: Fastback 402, Phi Delta Kappa Educational Foundation, 1996).

(and/or least) admire?" Collect individual responses to the question, tally, and discuss. After you have done this for several years, you may wish to share with your class for discussion purposes the results of your surveys of previous years.

78. Start a sister class program. Establish a class relationship with another similar class from another school from around the country or the world, perhaps by using the Internet.

79. During their study of westward expansion, challenge students to organize a role-play of a simulated family movement to the West in the 1800s. What items would they take? What would they throw out of the wagon to lighten the load?

80. Invite students to collect music, art, or athletic records from a particular period of history. Have them compare with today and predict the music, art, or records of the future.

81. Using play money, establish a capitalistic economic system within your classroom. Salaries may be paid for attendance and bonus income for work well done, taxes may be collected for poor work, and a welfare section may be established in a corner of the room.

82. Divide the class of students into small groups, and ask that each group make predictions as to what world governments, world geography, world social issues, or some other related topic will be like some time in the future. Let each group give its report, followed by debate and discussion. Plant the predictions in some secret location on the school grounds for a future discovery.

83. As opener to a unit on the U.S. Constitution, have students design their own classroom or team "bill of rights."

84. Initiate a service learning project, where for an extended period of time students work directly with community organizations.

85. Using Legos™ as construction blocks, over the course of most of the school year a history teacher at a Sacramento (California) high school has his ninth grade students simulate and role play the building of the Great Wall of China.

PAPER WORK: HOW TO AVOID BECOMING BURIED BY IT

A downfall for many beginning teachers is that of being buried under mounds of homework to be read and graded, leaving less and less time for effective planning. To prevent this from happening to you, consider the following suggestions.

Depending upon the purpose of the assignment, you will read student papers with varying degrees of intensity and scrutiny. If the purpose of the assignment is to assess mastery competence, then the papers should be read, marked, and graded only by you. On the other hand, for assignments that are designed for learning, understanding, and practice, you can have students check them themselves using either self-checking or peer-checking. During the self- or peer-checking, you can walk around the room, monitor the activity, and record whether a student did the assignment or not, or, after the checking, you can collect the papers and do a cursory review and your recording. Besides reducing the amount of paperwork for you, self- or peer-checking allows students to see and understand their errors, and it helps them develop self-evaluation techniques and standards.

PARENT AND GUARDIAN CONTACTS AND INVOLVEMENT

When parents (or guardians) are involved in their child's school and school work, students learn better and earn better grades, and teachers experience more positive feelings about teaching. Knowing this, schools increasingly are searching for new and better ways to involve parents (and even grandparents).

Some teachers make a point to contact parents or guardians by telephone or by electronic mail, especially when a student has shown a sudden turn for either the worse or the better in academic achievement or in classroom behavior. That initiative by the teacher is usually welcomed by parents and can lead to productive conferences with the teacher. A telephone conference can save valuable time for both you and the parent.

Another way of contacting parents is by letter. Contacting a parent by letter gives you time to think and to make clear your thoughts and concerns to that parent and to invite the parent to respond at her or his convenience by letter, by phone, or by arranging to have a conference with you.

Back-to-School Night and Open House

You will meet some of the parents or guardians early in the school year during "Back-to-School" or "Meet-the-Teacher" night and throughout the year in individual parent conferences and later in the year during open house. For the beginning teacher, these can be anxious times. But, in fact, it is a time to celebrate your work and to solicit help from parents.

Back-to-School night is the evening early in the school year when parents (and guardians) come to the school and meet their children's teachers. The parents arrive at the student's homebase and then proceed through a simulation of their sons' or daughters' school day; as a group, they meet each class and each teacher for a few minutes. Later, in the spring, there is an "open house" where parents may have more time to talk individually with teachers, although the major purpose of the "open house" is for the school and teachers to celebrate the work and progress of the students for that year. Throughout the school year, there will be opportunities for you and parents to meet and to talk about their child.

At Back-to-School night, parents are anxious to learn as much as they can about their children's teachers. You will meet each group of parents for a brief time, perhaps about ten minutes. During that meeting, you will provide them with a copy of the course syllabus (if an upper grade teacher), make some straightforward remarks about yourself, and talk about the course, its requirements, your expectations of the students, and how the parents might help.

Although there will be precious little time for questions from the parents, during your introduction the parents will be delighted to learn that you have your program well planned, are a "task master," appreciate their interest and welcome their inquiries and participation, and will communicate with them.

Specifically, parents will expect to learn about your curriculum—goals and objectives, any long-term projects, when tests will be given and if given on a regular basis, and your grading procedures. They will want to know what you expect of them: Will there be homework, and if so, should they help their children with it? How can they contact you? Try to anticipate other questions. Your principal, department chair, or colleagues can be of aid in helping you anticipate and prepare for these questions. Of course, you can never prepare for the question that comes from left field. Just remain calm and avoid being flustered (or at least appear to be calm). Ten minutes will fly by quickly, and parents will be reassured to know you are an in-control person.

Conferences

When meeting parents for conferences, you should be as specific as possible when explaining to a parent the progress of that parent's child in your class. And, again, express your appreciation for their interest. Be helpful to his or her understanding, and don't saturate the parent with more information than he or she needs. Resist any tendency to talk too much. Allow time for the parent to ask questions. Keep your answers succinct. Never compare one student with another or with the rest of the class. If the parent asks a question for which you do not have an answer, tell the parent you will try to find an answer and will phone the parent as quickly as you can. And do it. Have the student's portfolio and other work with you during the parent conference so you can show the parent examples of what is being discussed. Also, have your grade book on hand, or a computer printout of it, but be prepared to protect from the parent the names and records of the other students.

Sometimes it is helpful to have a three-way conference, a conference with the parent, the student, and you, or a conference with the parent, the principal or counselor, and several or all of the student's teachers. If, especially as a beginning teacher, you would like the presence of an administrator at a parent-teacher conference as backup, don't be hesitant to arrange that.

Some educators prefer a student-led conference, arguing that "placing students in charge of the conference makes them individually accountable, encourages them to take pride in their work, and encourages student-parent communication about school performance." But, like most innovations in education, the concept of student-led conferences has its limitations—the most important of which perhaps is the matter of time.[9]

---

[9] D. W. Johnson and R. T. Johnson, "The Role of Cooperative Learning in Assessing and Communicating Student Learning," page 43 in T. R. Guskey (ed.), *Communicating Student Learning,* 1996 ASCD Yearbook (Alexandria, VA: Association for Supervision and Curriculum Development, 1996). Regarding the pros and cons of a student-led conference and for a conference organizer tool, see J. Bailey and J. McTighe, "Reporting Achievement at the Secondary Level: What and How," pages 137-139 in T. R. Guskey, op cit. See also L. Countryman and M. Schroeder, "When Students Lead Parent-Teacher Conferences," *Educational Leadership* 53(7):64-68 (April 1996).

Home-School Links

At some schools, through homework hotlines, parents have phone access to their children's assignment specifications and to their progress in their schoolwork, and parents with a personal computer and a modem have access to tutorial services to assist students with assignments.

Some schools and teachers hold workshops for parents, times when parents learn more about what their children are doing in school and how they can help them.[10]

Dealing with a Hostile Parent

Dealing with an angry or hostile parent or guardian can be scary for any teacher, but especially for a beginning teacher. Here are some guidelines for dealing with such hostility.

Remain calm in your discussion with the parent, allowing the parent to talk out his or her hostility while you say very little; usually, the less you say the better off you will be. What you do say must be objective and to the point of the child's work in your classroom. The parent may just need to vent frustrations that might have very little to do with you, the school, or even the child.

Avoid allowing yourself to be intimidated, put on the defensive, or backed into a verbal corner. If the parent tries to do so by attacking you personally, do not press your defense at this point. Perhaps the parent has made a point that you should take time to consider; this may be a good time to arrange for another conference with the parent for about a week later. In a follow-up conference, if the parent agrees, you may want to consider bringing in a mediator, such as another member of your teaching team, an administrator, or a school counselor or psychologist.

Avoid talking about other students; keep the conversation focused on this parent's child's progress. The parent is *not* or should not be your rival. You both share a concern for the academic and emotional well-being of the child. Use your best skills in critical thinking and problem solving, trying to focus the discussion by identifying the problem, defining it, and then arriving at some decision about how mutually to go about solving it. To this end you may need to ask for help from a third party, such as the child's school counselor. If agreed to by the parent, please take that step.

---

[10] See, for example, F.L. Holmes, "Saturday Science: A Model for Parents and Children," *Science and Children* 26-29 (January 1998).

POLITICS AT SCHOOL: BEST TO AVOID

Sometimes, because of philosophical differences, power struggles, and political tensions within a school staff, a beginning teacher's struggles can become clouded with issues other than the usual ones concerning curriculum and student behavior.[11] My advice: Develop as quickly as possible a support network, made up of both colleagues at school and friends outside of the school who can support you in your work. Try to stay out of political issues and power struggles. As a beginning teacher, you can't afford the time, alienation, or emotional drain that involvement might cause.

PROFESSIONAL ORGANIZATIONS: SELECT AND JOIN ONE

There are many professional organizations, general and discipline specific—local, statewide, and national—and their programs, publications, and services can be very valuable to a beginning teacher. Most have a web page on the Internet. I suggest that because as a first-year teacher you are probably far from being wealthy, you investigate carefully all the possibilities, then select and join one professional organization that you believe will be most helpful and supportive for your work as a beginning teacher. Annual membership in that one organization might cost you anywhere from only a few dollars to several hundred. You may be entitled to a reduced membership rate if you are an enrolled university student.

PROTECTING STUDENTS AND YOURSELF: LIABILITY AND SAFETY

You need to be aware of potential liability and safety issues that can arise, especially from chauffeuring students, admitting them into your home, or simply being alone with a student. To prevent problems, avoid doing any of those things.

To best protect your students, and yourself, you must be knowledgeable about legal guidelines for public school teaching and about teacher and student rights, be steadily alert for potential safety

---

[11] See, for example, P. Graham and L. Krippner, "The First Year—Two Perspectives," *English Journal* 84(2):26 (February 1995).

hazards, and be knowledgeable about what you should or should not do in an emergency situation. Beyond the brief presentation that follows, you will want to continue to increase your awareness about these matters by talking with experienced teachers, reading, and attending workshops or classes where these and related topics are addressed in detail for your particular grade level or discipline.

Title IX

Federal law Title IX of the Education Act Amendments of 1972, P.L. 92-318, prohibits any teacher from discriminating among students on the basis of their gender. In all aspects of school, male and female students must be treated the same. This means, for example, that a teacher must not pit males against females in a subject content quiz game—or for any other activity or reason. Further, no teacher, student, administrator, or other school employee should make sexual advances toward a student (i.e., touching or speaking in a sexual manner).

Students should be informed by their schools of their rights under Title IX, and they should be encouraged to report any suspected violations of their rights to the school principal or other designated person. Each school or district should have a clearly delineated statement of steps to follow in the process of protecting students' rights. More frequently now than ever before, students are exercising their rights to be free from sexual harassment from peers as well as from adults.

Teacher Liability and Insurance

You are probably protected by your school district against personal injury litigation (i.e., a negligence suit filed as the result of a student being injured at school or at a school-sponsored activity). However, you may want to investigate the extent of your tort (i.e., any private or civil wrong for which a civil suit can be brought) liability coverage. You may decide that the coverage provided by the district is insufficient. Additional liability coverage can be obtained through private insurance agents and through many of the larger national teacher's organizations.

Teachers sometimes find themselves in situations where they are tempted to transport students in their own private automobiles, such as for field trips and other off-campus activities. Before ever transporting students in your automobile—or in private automobiles driven by volunteer adults—you and other drivers should inquire from your insurance agents whether you have adequate automobile insurance liability coverage to do that and if any written permissions or release from liability is needed. My advice is simply to avoid using your own vehicle to transport students.

Inevitably, teachers take personal items to school—purses, cameras, compact disc players, and so on. It is unlikely that the school's insurance policy covers your personal items if stolen or damaged. A homeowner's or apartment renter's policy might. My advice is to avoid taking valuable personal items to school.

Child Abuse and Neglect

Child abuse and neglect (e.g., physical abuse, incest, malnutrition, improper clothing, and inadequate dental care) has become a grave matter of pressing national concern. *Teachers in all states are legally mandated to report any suspicion of child abuse.* It is a serious moral issue to not report such suspicion, and lawsuits have been brought against educators for negligence for not doing so. To report your suspicion of child abuse, you can telephone toll free 1-800-4-A-CHILD. Proof of abuse is not necessary. If you do report your suspicion, you are probably immune from a libel suit. Check your own state or local school district for details about (a) what is designated as child abuse, (b) to whom to report your suspicion, (c) how to report, and (d) the immunity or protection provided to a teacher who does report suspected child abuse.

Although physical abuse is the easiest to detect, other types of abuse and neglect can be just as serious. Generally, children who are abused or neglected (a) are below normal in height and weight, (b) exhibit destructive behaviors, (c) exhibit hyperactive or aggressive behavior, (d) exhibit short attention spans and lack of interest in school activities, (e) exhibit sudden and dramatic changes in behavior, (f) are fearful of everyone and everything, (g) are fearful of going home after school, (h) are fearful of their parents and other adults, (i) are frequently sick and absent from school, (j) are frequently tired and often fall asleep in class, (k) smell of alcohol, (l) are unclean, smelling of body wastes, (m) exhibit unexpected crying, (n) have unexplained lacerations and bruises, (o) are withdrawn from adult contact, and (p) are withdrawn from peer interaction.[12] A student who comes to your classroom abused or neglected needs to feel welcome and secure while in the classroom. For additional guidance in working with such a student, contact experts from your

---

[12] D. G. Gil, *Violence Against Children: Physical Child Abuse in the United States* (Cambridge, MA: Rand McNally, 1970).

local school district, the state department of education, or a nearby Children's Protective Services (CPS) agency.

First Aid and Medication

Accidents and resulting injuries to students while at school do occur. While doing a science laboratory experiment, a student is burned by an acid or a flame. In an English class, a student is injured by glass from a falling window pane when the teacher attempts to open a stuck window. While playing during recess on the school ground, a student falls and lands on a lawn sprinkler head that had remained upright although the water was off. Do you understand what you should do when a student under your supervision is injured?

First, you should give first aid *only* when necessary to save a limb or life. When life or limb are not at risk, then you should follow school policy by referring the student immediately to professional care. When immediate professional care is unavailable and you believe that immediate first aid is necessary, then you can take prudent action, as if you were that students parent or legal guardian. But you must always be cautious and knowledgeable about what you are doing so that you do not cause further injury.

Unless you are a licensed medical professional, you should *never* give medication to a minor, whether prescription or over-the-counter. Students who need to take personal medication should bring from home a written parental statement of permission and instructions. Under your supervision as the student's classroom teacher—or that of the school nurse (if there is one)—the student can then take the medicine. Most older students will administer their personal medicine between classes, and you will not be involved.

RECORDS: MAINTAIN DOCUMENTATION

If you are not an organized person, then become so as quickly as possible. If necessary, find a colleague who seems to be well organized and ask how it is done. You must maintain well-organized and complete records of student achievement. You may do this in a written record book or on an electronic record book. At the very least, the record book should include attendance and tardy records and all records of student scores on tests, homework, projects, and other assignments.

In addition, I advise you to maintain a log and written record with copies of everything you communicate to parents and to school personnel (e.g., administrator, counselor, or school nurse).

Worst Nightmare

One reason for maintaining records is to be prepared to defend yourself if accused of misbehavior by a student, perhaps in retribution for something you did. Here are two recent examples, each involving a teacher and eighth-grade students.

A male beginning teacher was accused first by one eighth-grade female student, then by five other female students who joined her, of unwanted staring at the girls—in effect, of sexual harassment. The student who initiated the accusation had been caught by the teacher twice the week before cheating in class on a test and on an assignment. In speaking of the teacher, she also had written in her journal, "Let's get this bozo." Although the teacher's documentation and a conference with the school principal and the girl's parents helped to resolve the matter quickly in the teacher's favor, it still was an anxious and very unsettling experience for the teacher, who, upon reflection, questioned whether he wanted to continue in the profession.

In another situation, after a beginning teacher had accused an eighth-grade student of forging notes from home, in retribution the student wrote on an assignment, "Let's get him out of here." The student's parents phoned the school principal complaining that the teacher had unfairly accused their daughter of dishonesty. In a conference with the teacher, principal, and student's parents, the issue was resolved when the teacher apologized for his accusation. However, the teacher had lost all rapport with this particular class. The bottom line: Never accuse a student of cheating unless you have absolute proof.

RELIABILITY: A GOOD TEACHER IS A RELIABLE TEACHER

Make no commitments you cannot fulfill. You want to be considered as a person who is reliable, who can be relied on to fulfill professional responsibilities, promises, and commitments. A teacher who cannot be relied on is quick to lose credibility with the students (as well as with colleagues and administrators). An unreliable teacher is an incompetent teacher. And, for whatever reason, a teacher who is chronically absent from his or her teaching duties is an at-risk teacher—that is, one who is on the verge of dropping out of the profession.

SALARY: NOT GREAT BUT STEADY

Sometimes beginning teachers become disenchanted with their career choice because of the beginning salary, which for some is impossible to live on, especially for the teacher who has a family to support. Unfortunately, a beginning teacher with a family to support may have to moonlight to support his or her teaching income, and that takes time and energy from the teacher's devotion to teaching.

Beginning teacher salaries are dismal, as they always have been in this country, with society expecting much more from beginning teachers than it has ever been willing to pay for. However, the news is not all bad. The good news is that your income will very likely be steady, coming in every month, and will grow throughout your career, which may be for 30 or more years. Teachers are seldom laid off or fired; even, unfortunately, those who are grossly incompetent. In addition, many teachers are able to supplement their regular teaching income with additional income from summer or inter-session teaching or other school-related tasks.

A SENSE OF HUMOR, AN INTELLIGENT BEHAVIOR: PLEASE SMILE BEFORE CHRISTMAS

Students appreciate and learn more from a teacher who shares a sense of humor and laughs with the students. So, please smile before Christmas.

The positive effects of appropriate humor (i.e., humor that is not self-deprecating or disrespectful of others) on learning and living are well established: drop in the pulse rate; reduction of feelings of anxiety, tension, and stress; secretion of endorphins; and an increase in blood oxygen. Humor and laughter increases immune system activity and decreases stress-producing hormones. It causes an increase in the activity of the body's natural cells that attack and kill tumor cells and viruses. It activates T-cells for the immune system, antibodies that fight against harmful microorganisms, and gamma interferon, a hormone that fights viruses and regulates cell growth. Because of these effects, humor relaxes us and encourages creativity and higher level thinking. Humor is an intelligent behavior that should be cherished and nourished.

STUDENT LEARNING: WHEN CHILDREN DO NOT LEARN THE WAY WE TEACH THEM, THEN WE MUST TEACH THEM THE WAY THEY LEARN

So advises researcher and author Rita Dunn.[13] Learning modality refers to the sensory portal means (or input channel) by which a student prefers to receive sensory reception (modality preference) or the actual way a student learns best (modality adeptness). Some students prefer learning by seeing, a visual modality; others prefer learning through instruction from others (through talk), an auditory modality; while many others prefer learning by doing and being physically involved, referred to as kinesthetic modality, and by touching objects, the tactile modality. Sometimes a student's modality preference is not that student's modality strength.

While primary modality strength can be determined by observing students, it can also be mixed, and it can change as the result of experience and intellectual maturity. As one might suspect, *modality integration* (i.e., engaging more of the sensory input channels, using several modalities at once or staggered) has been found to contribute to better achievement in student learning.

Because many young people neither have a preference nor a strength for auditory reception, teachers should severely limit their use of the lecture method of instruction. Furthermore, instruction that uses a singular approach, such as auditory (e.g., lecturing to the students), cheats students who learn better another way. This difference can affect student achievement. A teacher, for example, who only lectures to the students or uses discussions day after day is shortchanging the education of children who learn better another way, who are, for example, kinesthetic and visual learners.

As a general rule, students prefer and learn best by touching objects, by feeling shapes and textures, by interacting with each other, and by moving things around. In contrast, learning by sitting and listening are difficult for many of them.

Students at Risk

Learning characteristics are known that significantly discriminate between students who are at risk of not finishing school and students who perform well. Students who are underachieving and at risk need (a) frequent opportunities for mobility, (b) options and choices, (c) a

---

[13] R. Dunn, *Strategies for Educating Diverse Learners* (Bloomington, IN: Fastback 384, Phi Delta Kappa Educational Foundation, 1995), p. 30.

variety of instructional resources, environments, and sociological groupings, rather than routines and patterns, (d) to learn during late morning, afternoon, or evening hours, rather than in the early morning, (e) informal seating, rather than wooden, steel, or plastic chairs, (f) low illumination, because bright light contributes to hyperactivity, and (g) tactile/visual introductory resources reinforced by kinesthetic (i.e., direct experiencing and whole-body activities)/visual resources, or introductory kinesthetic/visual resources reinforced by tactile/visual resources.[14]

You are advised to use strategies that integrate the modalities. When well designed, thematic units and project-based learning incorporate modality integration. In conclusion, then, when teaching a group of students of mixed learning abilities, mixed modality strengths, mixed language proficiency, and mixed cultural backgrounds, for the most successful teaching the integration of learning modalities is a must.

Learning Style Is Not an Indicator of Intelligence but of How a Person Learns

Related to learning modality is learning style, which can be defined as *independent forms of knowing and processing information*. While some older children may be comfortable with beginning their learning of a new idea in the abstract (e.g., visual or verbal symbolization), most need to begin with the concrete (e.g., learning by actually doing it). Many students prosper while working in groups, while others prefer to work alone. Some are quick in their studies, whereas others are slow and methodical and cautious and meticulous. Some can sustain attention on a single topic for a long time, becoming more absorbed in their study as time passes. Others are slower starters and more casual in their pursuits but are capable of shifting with ease from subject to subject. Some can study in the midst of music, noise, or movement, whereas others need quiet, solitude, and a desk or table. The point is this: *Students vary not only in their skills and preferences in the way knowledge is received, but also in how they mentally process that information once it has been received.* This latter is a person's style of learning. It is "a gestalt combining internal and external operations derived from the individual's neurobiology, personality, and development and reflected in learner behavior."[15]

---

[14] R. Dunn, *Strategies for Educating Diverse Learners*, p. 9.

[15] J. W. Keefe and B. G. Ferrell, "Developing a Defensible Learning Style Paradigm," *Educational Leadership* 48(2):59 (October 1990).

It is important to understand that *learning style is not an indicator of intelligence, but rather an indicator of how a person learns.* Although, as implied in the preceding paragraph, there are probably as many types of learning styles as there are individuals, David Kolb describes two major differences in how people learn: how they perceive situations and how they process information.[16] On the basis of perceiving and processing and the earlier work of Carl Jung, [17] Bernice McCarthy describes four major learning styles:[18]

- The *imaginative learner* perceives information concretely and processes it reflectively. Imaginative learners learn well by listening and sharing with others, integrating the ideas of others with their own experiences. Imaginative learners often have difficulty adjusting to traditional teaching, which depends less on classroom interactions and students' sharing and connecting of their prior experiences. In a traditional classroom, the imaginative learner is likely to be an at-risk student.

- The *analytic learner* perceives information abstractly and process it reflectively. The analytic learner prefers sequential thinking, needs details, and values what experts have to offer. Analytic learners do well in traditional classrooms.

- The *common sense learner* perceives information abstractly and processes it actively. Common sense learners are pragmatic and enjoy hands-on learning. They sometimes find school frustrating unless they can see immediate use to what is being learned. In the traditional classroom the common sense learner is likely to be a learner who is at risk of not completing school, of dropping out.

- The *dynamic learner* perceives information concretely and processes it actively. The dynamic learner also prefer hands-on learning and is excited by anything new. Dynamic learners are risk takers and are frustrated by learning if they see it as being tedious and

---

[16] D. A. Kolb, *The Learning Style Inventory* (Boston, MA: McBer, 1985). See also D. A. Kolb, *Experiential Learning: Experience as the Source of Learning and Development* (Upper Saddle River, NJ: Prentice Hall, 1984).

[17] C. G. Jung, *Psychological Types* (New York: Harcourt Brace, 1923). See also A. Gregorc, *Gregorc Style Delineator* (Maynard, MA: Gabriel Systems, 1985) and R. Dunn and K. Dunn, *Teaching Students Through Their Individual Learning Styles* (Reston, VA: Reston Publications, 1978).

[18] See B. McCarthy, "A Tale of Four Learners: 4MAT's Learning Styles," *Educational Leadership* 54(6):47-51 (March 1997).

sequential. In a traditional classroom the dynamic learner also is likely to be an at-risk student.

The Learning Cycle

To understand conceptual development and change, researchers in the 1960s developed a Piaget-based theory of learning, where students are guided from concrete, hands-on learning experiences to the abstract formulations of concepts and their formal applications. This theory became known as the three-phase learning cycle.[19] Long a popular strategy for teaching science, the learning cycle can be useful in other disciplines as well.[20] The three phases are (1) the *exploratory hands-on phase*, where students can explore ideas and experience assimilation and disequilibrium that lead to their own questions and tentative answers; (2) the *invention* or *concept development phase*, where, under the guidance of the teacher, students invent concepts and principles that help them answer their questions and reorganize their ideas, that is, the students revise their thinking to allow the new information to fit; and (3) the *expansion* or *concept application phase*, another hands-on phase, where the students try out their new ideas by applying them to situations that are relevant and meaningful to them. During application of a concept the learner may discover new information that causes a change in the learner's understanding of the concept being applied. Thus, the process of learning is cyclical.

There have been more recent interpretations or modifications of the three phase cycle, such as McCarthy's 4MAT.[21] With the 4MAT system, teachers employ a learning cycle of instructional strategies to try and reach each student's learning style. As stated by McCarthy, in the cycle learners "sense and feel, they experience, then they watch, they reflect, then they think, they develop theories, then they try out theories, they experiment. Finally, they evaluate and

---

[19] See R. Karplus, *Science Curriculum Improvement Study,* Teacher's Handbook (Berkeley: University of California, 1974).

[20] See, for example, A. C. Rule, *Using the Learning Cycle to Teach Acronyms, a Language Arts Lesson* (ED383000, 1995); J. E. Sowell, "Approach to Art History in the Classroom," *Art Education* 46(2):19-24 (March 1993); and T. O. Erb, "Teaching Diverse Students: Focus on the Learning Cycle," *Schools in the Middle* 4(1):16-20 (September 1994).

[21] For information about 4MAT, contact Excel, Inc., 23385 W. Old Barrington Road, Barrington, IL 60010 (847-382-7272), or at 6322 Fenworth Ct., Agoura Hills, CA 91301 (818-879-7442). For a description and sample lesson plans using the 4MAT model, see the Internet at <http://www.excelcorp.com/lessonCatalog.html>.

synthesize what they have learned in order to apply it to their next similar experience. They get smarter. They apply experience to experiences."[22] And, in this process, they are likely to be using all four learning modalities.

To evince *constructivist learning theory*, that is, that learning is a process involving the active engagement of learners, who adapt the educative event to fit, and expand, their individual world view (as opposed to the behaviorist pedagogical assumption that learning is something done to learners)[23] and to accentuate the importance of student self-assessment, some recent variations of the learning cycle include a fourth phase, an "assessment phase." However, because I believe that assessment of what students know or think they know should be a continual process, permeating all three phases of the learning cycle, I reject any treatment of "assessment" as a self-standing phase.

Learning Capacities

In contrast to four learning styles, Gardner introduces what he calls "learning capacities" exhibited by individuals in differing ways.[24] Originally and sometimes still referred to as multiple intelligences, capacities thus far identified are the following:

- *Bodily/kinesthetic*: ability to use the body skillfully and to handle objects skillfully
- *Interpersonal*: ability to understand people and relationships
- *Intrapersonal*: ability to assess one's emotional life as a means to understand oneself and others

---

[22] B. McCarthy, "Using the 4MAT System to Bring Learning Styles to Schools," *Educational Leadership* 48(2):33 (October 1990).

[23] R. DeLay, "Forming Knowledge: Constructivist Learning and Experiential Education," *Journal of Experiential Education* 19(2):76-81 (August/September 1996). See also "Constructivist Teaching" in J. W. Dougherty, *Four Philosophies That Shape the Middle School* (Bloomington, IN: Fastback 410, Phi Delta Kappa Educational Foundation, 1997).

[24] For Gardner's distinction between "learning style" and the "intelligences," see H. Gardner, "Multiple Intelligences: Myths and Messages," *International Schools Journal* 15(2):8-22 (April 1996); V. Ramos-Ford and H. Gardner, "Giftedness from a Multiple Intelligences Perspective," Chapter 5 of N. Colangelo and G. A. Davis (eds.), *Handbook of Gifted Education*, 2nd ed. (Needham Heights, MA: Allyn & Bacon, 1997); and the many articles in the "Teaching for Multiple Intelligences" theme issue of *Educational Leadership* 55(1) (September 1997).

- *Logical/mathematical*: ability to handle chains of reasoning and to recognize patterns and orders
- *Musical*: sensitivity to pitch, melody, rhythm, and tone
- *Naturalist*: ability to draw on materials and features of the natural environment to solve problems or fashion products
- *Verbal/linguistic*: sensitivity to the meaning and order of words
- *Visual/spatial*: ability to perceive the world accurately and to manipulate the nature of space, such as through architecture, mime, or sculpture[25]

As discussed above, many educators believe that many of the students who are at risk of not completing school are those who may be dominant in a cognitive learning style that is not in sync with traditional teaching methods. Traditional methods are largely of McCarthy's analytic style, where information is presented in a logical, linear, sequential fashion, and of three of the Gardner types: verbal/linguistic, logical/mathematical, and intrapersonal. Consequently, to better synchronize methods of instruction with learning styles, some teachers and schools have restructured the curriculum and instruction around Gardner's learning capacities. See the vignette in Figure 4.

SUBJECT KNOWLEDGE: FOUNTAINHEAD OF INFORMATION OR AN EDUCATIONAL BROKER?

It is common for beginning teachers to worry that they will be caught by students not knowing something in the field in which they are teaching. And indeed sooner or later you will be caught. But when that happens, use it as a teachable, not an embarrassing, moment.

Without question, you need to be knowledgeable about the subject matter content you have been hired to teach. You should have both historical understanding and current knowledge of the structure of those subjects you are expected to teach and of the facts, principles, concepts, and skills needed for those subjects. This doesn't mean you need to know everything about the subject, but more than you are likely to teach.

---

[25] See H. Gardner and T. Hatch, "Multiple Intelligences Go to School: Educational Implications of the Theory of Multiple Intelligence," *Educational Researcher* 18(8):4-9 (November 1989); and T. Blythe and H. Gardner, "A School for All Intelligences," *Educational Leadership* 47(7):33-37 (April 1990).

In one seventh-grade classroom, during one week of a six-week thematic unit on weather, students were concentrating on learning about the water cycle. For this study of the water cycle, with the students' help the teacher divided the class into several groups of three to five students per group. While working on six projects simultaneously to learn about the water cycle, (1) one group of students designed, conducted, and repeated an experiment to discover the number of drops of water that can be held on one side of a new one-cent coin versus the number that can be held on the side of a worn one-cent coin; (2) working in part with the first group, a second group designed and prepared graphs to illustrate the results of the experiments of the first group; (3) a third group of students created and composed the words and music of a song about the water cycle; (4) a fourth group incorporated their combined interests in mathematics and art to design, collect the necessary materials, and create a colorful and interactive bulletin board about the water cycle; (5) a fifth group read about the water cycle in materials they researched from the Internet and various libraries; and (6) a sixth group created a puppet show about the water cycle. On Friday, after each group had finished, the groups shared their projects with the whole class.

Figure 4: Classroom vignette: Using the theory of learning capacities (multiple intelligences) and multilevel instruction

Rather than a fountainhead of knowledge, view yourself as an "educational broker." You know where and how to discover information about content you are expected to teach. You cannot know everything there is to know about each subject, but you should become knowledgeable about where and how to best research it and how to assist your students in developing some of those same skills.

Teaching Out of Major for All or a Portion of the School Day: A Misuse and Abuse of Beginning Teachers

It is amazing and depressing when I learn of yet another first-year secondary school teacher being hired to teach at least part of the time out of his or her major field. Of all persons, the first-year teacher should not have to do this. The first year is demanding enough without having to struggle outside one's subject expertise.

If this happened to you, then don't be afraid to admit to the students that there are things about the subject that you do not know but, when they arise, that you and they will learn them together. View yourself as an expert on organizing for learning, as a confident and knowledgeable educational broker.

SUPPLIES AND TEXTBOOKS:
SELDOM ADEQUATE

Be prepared for the fact that basic supplies, such as paper, may be inadequate and depleted before the end of the school year. Insufficient and/or inadequate teaching supplies is a very real and common problem for beginning teachers (and veteran teachers, too), especially for those eager to involve the students in hands-on (doing it) and minds-on (thinking about what one is doing) learning.

Teachers find various creative although seldom permanent and satisfactory solutions to the problem of shortage of supplies, such as by publishing a wish list and sending it home with the children or sending it out on the school's web page, finding free resources from sources on the Internet, finding less expensive substitute materials, getting help from the parent-teacher organization or a community agency, holding a class fund-raiser such as a car wash, and applying for and receiving project grants. Talk with your colleagues about your teaching needs. When it comes to obtaining resources from the school administration, a group of teachers usually may have more clout than will an individual.

It is an unfortunate fact of life that good teachers have to resort to becoming scavengers and hoarders and to using their own money for the purchase of teaching materials. For a beginning teacher on a skimpy salary who may be still paying off college loans, this can be a nefarious situation.

What You Want for Your Birthday

It certainly is bold and probably erroneous for me to think that I should be able to tell you what it is that you want this year for your birthday, but consider this anyway. You may wish to inform relatives and significant others that this year for your birthday and other gift giving times, you prefer receiving materials and supplies that will enhance your teaching. To that end, you may want to prepare and provide them with a want/need list with sources and prices. For example, perhaps rather than a new sweater or item of jewelry, you would prefer a laser pointer, computer gradebook software, a ream of copy paper, a filing cabinet, or a large bag of crayons.

Student Textbooks

Generally speaking, students benefit by having their own copies of a textbook and in the latest edition. However, because of budget constraints, this may not always be possible. The book may be outdated; quantities may be limited. When the latter is the case, students may not be allowed to take the books home or perhaps may only occasionally do so. In other classrooms, there may be no textbook at all. Yet still, in some classrooms we have visited recently, there are two sets of the textbook, one set that remains in the classroom for use there and the other set that is assigned to students to take home and leave there for home studying. With that arrangement, students don't have to carry heavy books around in their backpacks. Among schools around the country, and for one reason or another, there are clearly the haves and the have nots.

Whatever your own situation, the following guidelines apply to using the textbook as a learning tool. Progressing through a textbook from the front cover to the back in one school term is not necessarily an indicator of good teaching. The textbook is one resource; to enhance their learning, students should be encouraged to use a variety of resources. Encourage students to search additional sources to update the content of the textbook. This is especially important in certain disciplines such as science and social sciences, where the amount of new information is growing rapidly and student's may have textbooks that are several years old. The library and sources on the Internet should be researched by students for the latest information on certain subjects. Keep supplementary reading materials for student use in the classroom. School and community librarians and resource specialists usually are delighted to cooperate with teachers in the selection and provision of such resources.

Consider differentiated reading and assignments in the textbook and several supplementary sources (see multireadings approach below). Except to make life simpler for the teacher, there is no advantage in all students working out of the same book and exercises. Some students benefit from the drill, practice, and reinforcement afforded by workbooks that accompany textbooks, but this is not true for all students, nor do all benefit from the same activity. In fact, the traditional workbook, now nearly extinct, is being replaced by the modern technology afforded by computer software and laser discs. As the cost of hardware and software programs becomes more realistic for schools, the use of computers by individual students is also becoming more common. Computers and other interactive media provide students with a psychologically safer learning environment in which they have greater control over the pace of the instruction, can repeat instruction if necessary, and can ask for clarification without the fear of having to do so publicly.

To help students develop their higher-level thinking skills and their comprehension of expository material, teach them how to study from their textbook, perhaps by using the SQ4R method:

> *Survey* the chapter, ask *questions* about what was read, *read* to answer the questions, *recite* the answers, *record* important items from the chapter into their notebooks, then *review* it all.

Encourage students to be alert for errors in the textbook, both in content and printing, by giving them some sort of credit reward, such as points, when they bring an error to your attention. This helps students develop the skills of critical reading, critical thinking, and healthy skepticism.

Rather than a single textbook approach, some teachers use a strategy that incorporates many readings for a topic during the same unit. This multireading strategy gives students a choice in what they read. The various readings provide some individualization of instruction by allowing for differences in reading ability and interest level. By using a study guide, all the students can be directed toward specific information and concepts, but they do not have to all read the same selections.

TEACHER'S LOUNGE: YOU MAY WANT TO AVOID IT

Teaching can be a highly stressful occupation. Because of that, teachers need sometimes to vent their frustrations. One place they do that is in the teacher's lounge. In order to not become sucked into the frequently negative clime that can permeate a teacher's lounge, wisely you may choose to stay out of it. And, when you do hear teachers complaining about students or administrators or parents or colleagues, walk away from the conversation.

TOTAL SCHOOL: YOU SHOULD GET INTO IT

Knowing that ultimately each and every activity has an effect upon the classroom, you will want to gradually assume an increasing active interest in total school life. The purpose of the school is to serve the education of the students, and the classroom is the primary, but not only, place where this occurs. Every committee meeting, school event, faculty meeting, school board meeting, office, program, and any other planned function that is related to school life shares in the ultimate purpose of better serving the education of the students. Unfortunately, too often adults forget this simple fact. You share in the task of reminding those that do forget.

Student Activities: There Is More to Teaching and Learning Than Classroom Work

There is always need for teachers to help with student activities that extend beyond the classroom, that is, with extracurricular matters, a few of which may offer extra money as incentive for the teacher volunteer. Although involvement in student activities is an excellent way to get to know and to establish rapport with students, beginning teachers sometimes underestimate the amount of time needed for the daily preparation for teaching, thereby overestimating how much time there will be left for extra assignments. During your first year, exercise wisdom and caution when volunteering for or agreeing to extra assignments, especially those that involve parents, student travel, or extensive financial matters. For example, being faculty sponsor for the school's chess club is probably less demanding and complicated than is being the faculty supervisor of the school newspaper or the school web page.

TRANSITIONS: A DIFFICULT SKILL TO MASTER

Transitions are the moments in lessons between activities or topics, or times of change. It will probably take a while for you to master the skill of smooth and meaningful transitions. Planning and consistency are important to your mastering this important skill. With a dependable schedule and consistent routines, transitions usually occur efficiently and automatically, without disruption. Still, research suggests that the greatest number of discipline problems occur during times of transitions, especially when students must wait for the next activity. To avoid problems during transitions, eliminate wait times by thinking and planning ahead. During the preactive phase (planning stage) of instruction, plan your transitions and write them into your lesson plan.

Transitions in lessons are of two types; in a transition one or both can be used. One type, called a lesson transition, is the way that the teacher connects one activity to the next so that students understand both the relationship between the two activities and the procedure for moving from one activity to the next with the least amount of confusion and wasted time.

The second type occurs when some students have finished a learning activity but must wait for others to catch up before starting the next. This type of transition we call an *anchor transitional activity* or, simply, anchor activity. The anchor activity is an activity that is intended to keep all students academically occupied, or anchored to a task, allowing no time where students have nothing to do but wait. A common example is when some students have finished a test but others have not. The effective teacher plans an anchor activity and gives instructions or reminders for that activity before students start the test or whatever the learning activity might be.

You can plan a variety of anchor activities relevant and appropriate to the topics being studied, although not necessarily related to the next activity of that particular lesson. Transitional activities may include any number of meaningful activities such as journal writing, worksheet activity, lab reports, portfolio work, homework, project work, and even work on an assignment for another class.

YOUR PLACE OF WORK: PLEASE SHOW PRIDE IN IT

A drab and uninteresting classroom usually reflects a drab and boring teacher. To the extent possible, you should make your classroom, that is, your place of work, an attractive and functional place to work and in which to learn. If you share a classroom with other teachers then you will need to talk with those teachers about the room and reach some agreement on how it will be shared.

YOUR FIRST OBSERVATION BY AN ADMINISTRATOR: HOW TO AVOID A PANIC ATTACK

Along about midyear, your teaching will be observed during a prearranged classroom visit by a school administrator, probably the school principal. This classroom observation will be followed closely by an evaluation post-conference and the principal's recommendation for your re-employment. As a beginning teacher, you undoubtedly will be anxious about this ensuing observation and evaluation. Just be prepared, confident, and proud.

Sometimes busy administrators, for one reason or another, must reschedule their visit to your classroom. This notice may come to you at the last minute, after you have carefully and thoughtfully prepared for the visit, both mentally and physically. For a beginning teacher, this can be very disappointing. In my opinion, once an observational visit is scheduled, except for a dire emergency, it should remain paramount in an administrator's schedule. Administrators sometimes forget how anxious a beginning teacher can become over the first evaluative observation.

If you confidently and consistently follow the guidelines and suggestions that have been presented in this booklet, the evaluation should go very much in your favor. Use the observational visit as an opportunity to display pride in your work and in your place of work; it will, unfortunately, likely be one of only a handful of times during your entire teaching career that an adult colleague visits your classroom to observe your work.

SUMMARY

As a teacher, you are a learner among learners. This is the beginning of an important career, during which you will be in a perpetual mode of reflection and learning. During your first year, you should not expect mastery from yourself. Rather, establish some realistic and achievable goals for yourself and then work toward those goals, periodically reflecting and self-assessing on both what and how you are doing. Experience and learn, and before you know it you will be recognized by your students, parents, and colleagues as a master teacher.

Teaching is variously referred to as an act of mercy, a performing art, a moral craft, and a science. Surely, good teaching is as much an art as it is a science. There is no magic bag of recipes that one experienced in such matters can pass on to beginners that will always work in every situation. You are a teacher, not a chef. Starting now and continuing throughout your career, you will try your own ideas and you will borrow ideas from others. You will continue to discover what works best for you in your own distinct situation with your own unique set of students.

I am indebted and grateful to all the people in my life, now and in the past, who have interacted with me and reinforced what I have felt since the days I first began my career as teacher: Teaching is the most rewarding profession of all. Best of luck to you for what can be a long-lasting and very rewarding career.

Richard D. Kellough

FOR FURTHER READING

Callahan, J. F.; Clark, L. H.; and Kellough, R. D. *Teaching in the Middle and Secondary Schools.* 6th ed. Upper Saddle River, NJ: Merrill/Prentice Hall, 1998.

Harmin, M. *Inspiring Active Learning: A Handbook for Teachers.* Alexandria, VA: Association for Supervision and Curriculum Development, 1994.

Kellough, R. D. *A Resource Guide for Teaching: K-12.* 2nd ed. Upper Saddle River, NJ: Merrill/Prentice Hall, 1997.

Kellough, R. D. and Kellough, N. G. *Middle School Teaching: A Guide to Methods and Resources.* 3d ed. Upper Saddle River, NJ: Merrill/Prentice Hall, 1999.

Kellough, R. D. and Kellough, N. G. *Secondary School Teaching: A Guide to Methods and Resources.* Upper Saddle River, NJ: Merrill/Prentice Hall, 1999.

Kellough, R. D. and Roberts, P. L. *A Resource Guide for Elementary School Teaching: Planning for Competence.* 4th ed. Upper Saddle River, NJ: Merrill/Prentice Hall, 1998.

Kellough, R. D., et al. *Integrating Language Arts and Social Studies for Intermediate and Middle School Students.* Upper Saddle River, NJ: Merrill/ Prentice Hall, 1996.

Kellough, R. D., et al. *Integrating Mathematics and Science for Intermediate and Middle School Students.* Upper Saddle River, NJ: Merrill/ Prentice Hall, 1996.

Kellough, R. D., et al. *Integrating Mathematics and Science for Kindergarten and Primary Children.* Upper Saddle River. NJ: Merrill/ Prentice Hall, 1996.

Miller, J. A. "Doing Whatever It Takes." *Education Week* (17)17:48-50 (January 8, 1998).

Roberts, P. L. and Kellough, R. D. *A Guide to Developing an Interdisciplinary Thematic Unit.* Upper Saddle River, NJ: Merrill/Prentice Hall, 1996.

Roberts, P. L., et al. *Integrating Language Arts and Social Studies for Kindergarten and Primary Children.* Upper Saddle River, NJ: Merrill/Prentice Hall, 1996.

INDEX